ABOUT THE A

Born in 1994, Michael L. Slaughter is currently 21 years old and a senior at Sacred Heart University graduating in May 2016. He is a double major in accounting and finance with a 3.94 GPA, and he is a member on the Division 1 Men's Lacrosse Team. Michael is a Welch Scholar in the John F. Welch College of Business, which is an honor awarded to the top ten students at the University, and he has also received numerous other academic accolades. In addition, he helps teach finance students as well as mentor freshmen at Sacred Heart.

Michael is the founder and owner of his own business, "Tons of Cards and More." At the age of 10, he created his business with no idea where it would take him – he just had a dream, and the inspiration and drive to follow it. After establishing a prominent online brand on eBay and Amazon over numerous years, Michael took the risk of building his own website to further expand sales. With no prior experience or knowledge in web design, he spent over 1,500 hours throughout a six-month period creating and designing an e-commerce website to grow his business (www.tonsofcardsandmore.com). While attending college full-time, he continues to work over 50+ hours a week on his business alone. After 11 years of hard work and sleepless nights, Michael has positioned himself as one of the world's top sellers in his industry.

Lastly, Michael is very passionate about the financial markets, an interest which developed in his early teenage years. He is looking to continue his passion upon graduation by having a prominent career in this industry. In his free time, he enjoys exercising, surfing, fishing, and reading.

For business or speaking inquiries, please contact Michael at: mslaughter.business@gmail.com

From Failure to Triumph

From Failure to Triumph

Inspiring Stories to Help You Overcome
Challenges and Achieve Success

Michael L. Slaughter

From Failure to Triumph

Printed in the United States of America

ISBN: 978-0-9966049-0-1

ACKNOWLEDGMENT

I would like to acknowledge Laura Ho for her invaluable help with the book's layout and cover design. I truly appreciate her wisdom and guidance, and the opportunity to work with her.

I would like to thank my family for all their unconditional support throughout my life. Being someone who is very self-driven and loves to accept daunting challenges, I have often as a result faced many disappointments, and knowing I always have my family there to support me has been invaluable. I really want to say thank you to my mom, Linda; my dad, Craig; and my sister, Katie for all they have done for me.

Contents

Chapter 1

Introduction – My Main Purpose

This book was created out of my desire to encourage and inspire others to achieve their dreams. We all have dreams, whether consciously or subconsciously, and the path to success requires great courage and work. It is not easy but instead very difficult, and too often people give up during the process. We all need the inspiration to continue our pursuits, and sometimes the best way is to read about the struggles and challenges others have overcome in history.

Along the way to my personal successes, I faced unimaginable challenges that required significant energy and effort to conquer. The challenges we face on the road to accomplishing our dreams only help strengthen our desire for success, and it makes the reward of achieving our goal worth so much more. As you progress through your life and achieve your goals, you will develop a road map that you can use for any endeavor that you take on later in life. But there still comes a time, especially with your largest goals, where it seems the world is working against you; you feel as if everything that can go wrong is going wrong. You feel as though the world is a negative place filled with evil – you see the dark and feel discouraged.

You CANNOT think like this, and you must immediately change your mindset. The world is your mirror, and what you think is what you will see. If you think negatively, you will see only the negative aspects about life. You will focus on these despairing things and spin all positive events into negatives. If you think positively and are happy about life, you will see all the beneficial things life has to offer and you will in return be rewarded with more happiness. Think about the last time you were really happy, and think about how you perceived the outside world. Even if negative things happened to you, you did not let it affect you and you probably did not even notice that they were negative things.

Our minds are our most powerful weapon, and those individuals that realize this and use it to help themselves are the ones who have reached success. When you think negatively, it turns into a negative cycle that feeds upon itself. Here is how it works: let's say for example you want to lose weight. You think negatively about your goal of losing weight, and this causes you to take no action. You feel as though it is too hard or difficult to lose weight, or you think that you never see progress immediately so what is the point. This attitude causes you to not go to the gym, which in turn makes you remain in your initial state of being overweight. You then realize after a while that you have made no progress towards losing weight, and you think more negatively. Thus, the cycle repeats and you never make any progress.

Think about a situation where this has happened to you. It may actually be your weight loss goals, but it could also be your goal of doing better in the classroom, maintaining better relationships with your significant other or family members, or your personal goals of overcoming an addiction and growing spiritually.

The goal does not matter, but think about the situation and why you thought like this. Did you listen to the opinions of others? Did you feel self-conscious about the progress you made along the way and decided to give up? Were you not fully committed to your goal, but felt like you were accomplishing it to please someone else? You have to be honest as you will never make any progress lying to yourself. You have to understand how you think and why you do what you do.

Great accomplishments happen as the result of energy and effort. You have to be fully committed to your dreams and go after them with everything you have. You cannot be partially committed, or even committed, you have to be FULLY committed if you want to see results. Success is nothing more than many little tasks and accomplishments added together to form one large achievement. How do you climb a mountain? Is it with one giant step from the bottom to the top, or do you take many little steps that eventually result in you standing at the top? Each step seems insignificant as you climb that mountain. You will rationalize that a single step does not matter and that you can skip this workout, or skip this homework assignment, or continue your addiction for one more day. But doing so is the equivalent to running back down the mountain, not just walking down it. It is much easier to turn back to your old habits, than it is accomplishing a dream. When you continue your old habits for even one extra day, think of it as though you just ran down the mountain for one hour. You can still see the top, but you only just prolonged the hike and made it harder on yourself. Always remember, that even if you do everything in your power to be better each day, you will still face down moments. Just like a mountain is not a linear progression, there will be ups and downs within your life as you climb to the top.

I understand that you have other things going on in your life, or that you may not live in an ideal situation. You may have been bullied, lost friends, raised by a single parent, or faced difficult failures in the past, I understand. But you cannot keep reminiscing about these painful experiences, otherwise you will keep living this reality. You have to reflect on the situation, and put it behind you. Your past does not have to be your future. Just because you have failed many times in the past, and your life up to this point has been painful, does not mean it will continue to be this way unless you let it.

Think of something you have always dreamed of… it could be obtaining that degree, having a great relationship with your family, becoming rich, obtaining that dream job; think of what it is. Say right now out loud to yourself "My goal of (say your goal) is possible, and I understand that if I work hard at it with everything I have, the universe will reward me." And then follow with this line, "If others have done it, then I can do it too!"

The following chapters contain inspirational stories to help encourage and inspire you to achieve your goals. Even the most determined individuals will want to quit at times because they cannot see the light at the end of the tunnel, and it is in those times where your level of commitment will be tested. These stories you are about to read will help show you that success is challenging, but if you never give up, you will achieve your dreams. People think success was just given to successful individuals; that they in a sense never faced any difficult times in their lives. You will be greatly surprised by the failures that highly successful individuals have faced along their journeys, but they understood during the process that pain is temporary. If they quit, they would have never achieved their dream, and the whole world would have suffered as a result.

I have included stories about some of the most well-known individuals in our society to show you that EVERYONE faces difficulties and failures on his or her path to success. You can never let the failures consume you. For many of you, life has punched you square in the face. Are you going to accept that? Do you really want that to be your reality? Or are you going to get up and fight back? These individuals fought back with everything they had, and they developed a character that embraced failure as a part of the process to success.

Some stories will resonate with your life and your goals better than others, so re-read those stories the next time fear, doubt, or anxiety poisons your mind. Do whatever you can to fill your mind with positive thoughts. I cannot wait to see the success you will have.

Chapter 2

Thomas – A Non-Athletic Backup

Born in 1977, Thomas was his parents' only son. As a child, he attended San Francisco 49ers games watching Joe Montana (legendary quarterback of the 49ers at the time) play football. Thomas desired to one day be like his idol, Joe Montana, but multitudinous obstacles stood in his way from where he was to where he wanted to end up. Thomas would face extreme difficulties and setbacks along the way that would have caused anyone with the slightest amount of self-doubt or a weak desire to quit.

Thomas did not play football until his freshman year in high school, which for some is considered to be a very late start. He was the backup quarterback on his freshmen football team, which went 0-8 during the season. To make matters worse, Thomas never even played on the worst team in the league! He did not even possess the skill to play on the absolute worst team that could not even win a single game during the season. Thomas' competition for playing time on his team consisted of kids that could not even win one game all year, and even amongst these kids who had no skill, he still sat on the bench all season.

Instead of feeling discouraged and quitting football to see if he could be successful at another sport, Thomas spent his summer improving his skills so he could be prepared for the next season. At this point, many kids in a similar situation would have given up football in pursuit of finding a different sport where they could possibly have a chance of succeeding because their inner voice tells them they have no chance of ever being a great football player. It is very easy to listen to that critic within us that fills our mind with negative thoughts, but it is in these moments where our enthusiasm and internal fortitude are tested. If Thomas would have listened to his negative thoughts, this chapter would have never existed.

The following year as a sophomore in high school, Thomas was able to get playing time simply because the starting quarterback ahead of him on his freshman team that went 0-8 quit playing football. This other quarterback could not take the pain of losing every game and decided to move onto something else – he did not have the work ethic or desire to overcome his current situation, improve his game, and begin to have a winning season. Thomas had the mental fortitude, unlike the other quarterback, to change himself first in order for his team's circumstances to change.

Thomas' remaining years in high school were quite successful, but simply because he put in the effort each day. He would spend much of his days on the field or in the film room critiquing his game to ensure he would be ready for each and every moment ahead of him. If he instead chose to play video games or watch T.V. with his time, someone else on his team would have risen to the occasion and claimed that starting quarterback position.

Without effort and energy, there will be absolutely no progress. If Thomas had waited for his circumstances to change in order to change himself, he would have been waiting endlessly. Thomas' circumstance of being a backup quarterback would never change unless he did something first to change his skills. He realized he had to become better today than he was yesterday in order to be tomorrow what he is not today – and that meant improving his arm strength, throwing accuracy, endurance, and football intelligence. If Thomas kept doing what he always did, he would have kept getting what he had always got – and that was being a backup quarterback on the worst team in the league.

As a result of the countless hours he put into practicing on the field and in the weight room, Thomas earned a spot on the University of Michigan roster to play collegiate football at the highest level. This university is known for attracting some of the top talent in the country, so Thomas would now be in a position of actually competing against the best.

Arriving on campus, no one handed Thomas his dream of being a starting collegiate quarterback on a silver platter. Coming in as a freshman, he was at the bottom of the food chain, and in front of him would only be challenges. Even though Thomas kept improving his skills every day by working with the receivers, lifting in the weight room, and watching hours of film, it was not until his sophomore year that he was competing for the starting quarterback position.

By the end of his freshman year, Thomas put in an entire year's worth of work, and he had barely even touched the field. Game after game had passed by that freshman season and Thomas sat on the bench, but this did not discourage him in the slightest – he knew he had to put the work in first in order to achieve success later on.

During the preseason of his sophomore year, Thomas was tied for the starting position on the depth chart with an upperclassman quarterback. It was unknown to the team who would be declared the starter, but Thomas had great hopes that he would win the starting role. However, to Thomas' stern disappointment, the upperclassman quarterback was announced as the starter simply because of the coach's rule at the time, which was the upperclassman wins the starting spot in any situation where an underclassman and upperclassman are tied on the depth chart.

Imagine putting in all that effort, and being so close to tasting your first drop of success at the collegiate level, and you are not named the starting quarterback simply because the other player is older. What the coach and the starting upperclassman quarterback did not know was that this decision further created a fire within Thomas to prove his coach wrong and show him that he deserved to be the starting quarterback.

On your path to success, the hunger and desire to win has to be so intense that nothing will ever stop you. It does not matter what disappointment or challenge you face; your hunger has to be so strong that you overcome it. You must pour your entire heart into your endeavor, and you must tell yourself there is no other option but winning. You will not accept losing, failure, or defeat. It is either win or keep trying.

Thomas was able to finally earn that starting position over his next two seasons. He did not start as a quarterback until his junior year in college, in which he had a successful year. Once again, he had to EARN it. Nothing was ever given to him in his life, everything he achieved he had earned.

The following year as a senior, Thomas was named captain of the team. Even as a senior and a captain, he still faced intense competition for his starting quarterback spot. In his senior season, the coach wanted to replace him with a recruit who had just joined the team as a freshman – this player was viewed as the best recruit to ever come to Michigan. The coach worried that if the recruit did not play in his freshman year, he would transfer as a result. Thomas had to fight off both this new competition and the coach's desire to find reasons why the recruit should be a starter over him. While Thomas may have been first on the depth chart, he trained like he was second.

Often times, being in first place causes an individual to train just a little bit less because he gets too comfortable thinking he is best and his ego blocks that inner hunger to win. An individual who is in second place has such an overwhelming hunger not to come in second again, but to be first, that he will endure whatever it takes to be the winner. This is often the reason why teams who win championships have a difficult time repeating it the following year even though the team consists of exactly the same players.

Thomas was able to prove he deserved the starting spot in the beginning of the season after a few incredible performances on the field in the closest of games and under the loudest roars of opposing crowds. These are the moments where true athletes are tested – when the game is on the line, the crowd is screaming against you, and all odds of winning are not in your favor. It is very easy to allow your nerves and the immense pressure to control your performance in these critical final minutes, but Thomas' preparation in practice each week equipped him with the proper mindset to overcome these distractions and inner doubts during the game.

He had a stellar final season, and Thomas believed he would be drafted in the beginning rounds of the 2000 NFL draft. However, the recruiting reports on him by NFL scouts were extremely dismissive of his prospects as a professional quarterback. One report said "poor build, lacks great physical stature, lacks strength, lacks a strong arm, cannot throw a tight spiral, and gets knocked down easily." His 40-yard dash time was 5.2 seconds, which by NFL standards, is very slow. At a San Francisco 49ers training camp prior to the NFL draft, the coaches said that out of the 576 quarterbacks they have ever looked at in their years coaching, Thomas was ranked last.

Thomas was a "nobody" in the draft, no one had heard of him despite his successful career at a large university. He was not a household name, he did not have the best statistics, and he was not the best athlete. Michigan had wanted to replace him as the starting quarterback for multiple years, and his coach did not even sell him to the NFL coaches as the best player to come out of Michigan – Thomas did not even have his coach's support entering the NFL draft. But what was it that Thomas possessed that can be difficult to measure but so vitally important to success? And that is Thomas possessed enthusiasm, drive, and the heart of a champion.

Can you guess what happened? Like everything else in his life, he had to start at the bottom and work his way to the top. Six other quarterbacks would be drafted before him that year, and Thomas was eventually drafted as the 199th pick in the sixth round of the NFL draft by the New England Patriots. NFL coaches said he was "lucky" to even be drafted at all.

In his rookie year, Thomas met Robert Kraft, the owner of the Patriots. After Thomas introduced himself, Mr. Kraft said "I know who you are, you're our 6th round draft choice." And Thomas replied "That's right, I'm the best decision this organization ever made." Even though Thomas was an unknown and viewed by the NFL as a hopeless player, he had the self-confidence and belief in himself to tell the owner of the organization that this was their best decision ever. How many of you would have said this to the *owner* of a professional team, especially when you were viewed as being "lucky" to even be drafted?

Self-confidence is a critical ingredient to success. You can possess all the skills and attributes necessary to succeed in your particular field, but a lack of confidence will cause you to be unaware of your abilities and thus never put yourself in a position to excel because you will never engage in any action.

Thomas' level of confidence is the exact attribute you need to have when chasing your own dreams. Regardless of what the external world tells you, you need to internally tell yourself that you will make it. You need to realize your importance on this Earth and how critical it is to all of society that you achieve your goal. With the proper work ethic and the determination to never quit, your dream is possible.

During Thomas' rookie year, there were no signs that he would ever be successful in the league. He barely made the final roster after training camp that year and was listed as the fourth string quarterback. The coach of the New England Patriots, Bill Belichick, kept Thomas because he thought he could possibly, under the right offensive structure, become a better quarterback one day. From the time he became a New England Patriot, Thomas prepared for the moment in his professional career where he would eventually see the field. Even though he saw no evidence of ever having a chance to play in his rookie year, he prepared as if it was about to happen. He understood that failing to prepare is preparing to fail. Thomas did not ever want to be in a situation where he would be given an opportunity and not be ready for it.

Well the moment finally came for Thomas to show his worth. In 2001, the starting quarterback, Drew Bledsoe, got hurt in a pre-season game, and it was Thomas' chance to put all of his life's work into this one moment. And the result….Bledsoe never claimed his starting spot back again.

Thomas led the New England Patriots to a Super Bowl in his first-ever season playing as a starting quarterback in the NFL. He still plays to this day with a chip on his shoulder and the mindset that at any moment he could lose his starting position, and this has allowed him to push himself to new levels. He has made it to the Super Bowl six times in his career, winning four of them, and has been named the Super Bowl MVP three times. He is currently fifth on the all-time list for career passing yards and fifth for career touchdown passes. His playoff win total is the highest in NFL history, and he set the record for the longest consecutive win streak in the history of the NFL. He has thrown for more passing yards than any quarterback in the NFL postseason, and he will eventually be placed in the NFL Hall of Fame when he retires. So who is this quarterback that could not play on the worst team in league? Well, none other than Tom Brady.

"Too often in life, something happens and we blame other people for us not being happy or satisfied or fulfilled. So the point is, we all have choices, and we make the choice to accept people or situations or to not accept situations."
– Tom Brady

Chapter 3

Howard – From the Projects

Howard was born in 1953 and grew up as a child in a family of five. He lived in the Bayview Housing projects of Brooklyn, New York, and his mother and father greatly struggled financially to fulfill the basic needs of their family. A bullet hole in the glass marked the entrance to the building where Howard and his family struggled to survive. Howard's father was a high school dropout, a war veteran, and had a series of very-low paying blue collar jobs. As a child, Howard and his family did not even have the basic benefits of medical coverage, so the remedy to any sickness was just rest.

Your past and current circumstances have nothing to do with your future reality. The sooner you realize this the sooner you will begin to see success in your life. It is not your resources that matter – what matters is your resourcefulness. Our world has always been filled with the resources needed to be build skyscrapers, technological devices, and medical advancements, but it was not until certain individuals came along and were resourceful with what is provided to us on Earth that these final products were made.

A tragedy soon came upon their family when Howard was seven years old – his father lost his job as a diaper-service delivery driver after breaking his leg. This particular job, along with most blue-collar jobs, requires a worker to have a fully-functioning body. Without Howard's father being able to work due to a broken leg, all paychecks ceased. Already in a financially difficult situation, their circumstances only worsened over the next few months to where they became too poor to even afford food. It was during this despairing time, however, that Howard refused to ever live like this again. He turned all the pain from these unforgiving childhood years of watching his parents struggle into his greatest "why" for all his endeavors.

During his school years, his dream was to get out of the projects and live a better life. Being an athletic kid, he focused on football in high school and was able to earn a scholarship to play at Northern Michigan University. Coming from an impoverished family, this athletic scholarship was the only way Howard could have the opportunity to attend college. However, in his freshman year, Howard suffered an injury and had to quit the team because of it – his scholarship was now gone. Knowing an education was the only way out, he refused to succumb to the challenges life presented him. It would have been so easy for Howard to drop out of college because of his circumstances and the situation he now faced, but he decided he would do whatever it took to obtain a college education. With no financial support from his family and the loss of his scholarship, Howard had to occasionally sell his blood throughout college in order to pay tuition.

Now, think again when you say there is no way you can afford that college degree, or that there is no way you can pass that test. You need to think through challenges creatively because there will always be ways to overcome any obstacle. Do you value your dreams enough to donate blood in order to achieve them? Or how many of you would have even considered this in the first place? Most people would rather complain about their situation than take any action to change it, but that is why you do not want to be like most people. You are a unique asset to this world, and the legacy and impact you will leave on society will never be forgotten.

Upon his college graduation in 1975, Howard worked as a salesman at Xerox. While employed by this company, he learned through relentless experience the difficulties of cold-calling, and he began to develop a strong inner core that embraced failing as an unavoidable part of being a successful salesman. Like everything else up to this point in his life, he always put his best effort into any endeavor he undertook as the voice of his distraught father and the images of his childhood struggles were imprinted in his memory.

After being a standout salesman at Xerox, Howard was then recruited to become an appliance salesman at a company called Hammarplast. After climbing the hierarchical corporate ladder based on his performance, Howard noticed that Hammarplast was selling a lot of coffee makers to a small place in Seattle, Washington. In 1981, Howard visited this small shop which was founded in 1971 and sold only coffee beans, teas, and spices (not drinks).

Shortly after this visit, Howard took a job working at this small coffee shop because he felt an unexplainable feeling of "home" when he walked into the store for the first time. He listened to his little inner voice that called out to him that he needed to give up his career at Hammarplast and work at this coffee shop. Our inner voice tries to give us the right direction on where we should take our lives, but our minds often overpower it by rationalizing why we should stay where we currently are because of the risks and uncertainties associated with taking a risk.

While on vacation in Italy in 1983, Howard had an epiphany. He realized that coffee was an integral part of the Italian culture and not just something people casually drink like water, and that this cultural concept should be applied to the small coffee shop he was working at in Seattle. Excited and enthusiastic about his new idea, he went to the founders of the coffee shop in Seattle with his vision of implementing this type of cultural atmosphere in their shop. Their response was that this concept was not for them and should not be done at this store.

Not everyone is going to have your vision and see what you see, that is why it is your vision and not theirs. Just like I can show two people an illusionary picture and they will see two different images, it is no surprise that not everyone will see what you see, especially if your idea is revolutionary. People are going to tell you that your idea is not possible or that it is not going to work because the finished product of your idea is unknown to society at that time. Anything remarkable was viewed as being impossible before it was achieved. Society only accepts a feat as being possible after it is done and known to the world. The larger you dream, the less likely that anyone will support your vision. But it is your vision in the first place, so why care what they think?

Frustrated by the founders' lack of vision in his new idea for the shop, Howard left to create his own coffee shop in 1986 called Il Giornale. At this time, his wife was 6-7 months pregnant with their child, and his wife's father took Howard out on a long walk, and said to him "I want to ask you to do something and that is to give up this dream and hobby and get a job."

Howard could have easily listened to him because after all, this is the father of his wife, but a flame existed deep within him to pursue his dream and nothing or no one could put it out. Enthusiasm is one of the most dynamic qualities a person can possess because with an abundance of it, nothing that happens can possibly stop an individual from succeeding. With enthusiasm, you will always find a way.

In 1987, to Howard's surprise, the two founders of the small coffee shop in Seattle that he had previously worked at were looking to sell their place. In order to purchase this shop and merge it together with II Giornale, Howard would need a large amount of capital. Without the ability to pay for it from his own personal savings, he was only left with the option of having to take out a loan. Howard went from bank to bank sharing his concept and seeking a loan, but each one turned him down calling his idea ludicrous. All in all, Howard was turned down by 217 banks.

His idea of having a coffee shop with unusual drinks where customers would pay a high amount seemed preposterous to all of these banks. Why would anyone pay up for a cup of coffee when at the time it only cost $0.50? Coffee was viewed as being just simply a basic drink and not something sophisticated like wine. To make matters worse, at the time he was pitching his new concept, coffee consumption had been declining since 1962. The coffee market had been declining for over 25 years, so why would the demand for coffee suddenly rise AND cause consumers to want to purchase an expensive cup of it? Bank after bank tried to warn him about all the negatives, but Howard refused to listen to them. While 217 banks may have turned him down, a few banks finally agreed to loan him the money.

It does not matter how many times you face rejection, all it takes is one more attempt to have the possibility of being viewed as a success. Because let's face it, his mission of getting a loan was successful, was it not? Even though he faced insurmountable failures in the process, he achieved the end result he was after, and his efforts were successful.

How many of you would have the tenacity to visit the 218th bank? Let alone with the same enthusiasm and vigor that you possessed when you visited the first bank? After being turned down by a few banks, you would think Howard would have given up and believed the opinions of these financial experts, but he instead chose to believe in himself rather than the opinions of others.

If I could tell you right now that your dream will become a reality but only after you have committed 10 years of sacrifice lined with hours and hours of pain each day, would you still pursue it? Because that is what you will have to go through in order to achieve your dream. If you are just as enthusiastic as Howard, the sacrifice and pain will weigh very little compared to the weight of your grand success when you are given that diploma, win that championship, pass that test, or earn that promotion.

Howard finally merged the two coffee shops together in 1987, and his newly founded coffee shop would foster an environment that created human connection, conversation, and a sense of community. He continually worked at improving operations at his shop and expanding locations, but most importantly, Howard focused on treating his employees well beyond any standard in the restaurant industry. He provided his employees with many benefits including healthcare, to both full and part-time employees, and the ability to purchase stock options in the company once he took it public in 1992.

In the midst of the company's growth in 1996, Howard looked to expand his coffee shop internationally, and he chose Japan to be his first international location. The company hired top consultants to research the area and advise them on how to proceed. These consultants came back saying the company would not succeed in Japan and listed many problems with the area.

Just like Howard had done so many times in his life, he disregarded their advice and believed in his instincts. I am sure the critics felt quite foolish on opening day of his coffee shop in Japan in August of 1996 as hundreds waited for the grand opening, some even having slept outside the shop for days.

This man was Howard Schultz, the founder of Starbucks Coffee. Starbucks currently has more than 21,000 locations in 65 countries. Howard prides himself on the friendly service and atmosphere in all his locations, and he calls his employees "partners" because they are not just employees to the company, but partners with it. Starbucks is very environmentally friendly and it has been rated the #1 coffee retailer in the United States. Starbucks spends more on healthcare for part-time employees than it does on the total cost of actual coffee beans.

Howard Schultz has a net worth of more than $2.8 billion, and he has received countless awards such as the 2004 International Distinguished Entrepreneur Award, Fortune's 2011 Businessperson of the Year, the FIRST Responsible Capitalism Award, and many more.

From the projects of Brooklyn, New York to donating blood to afford college tuition and hearing 217 banks tell him "NO" to his dream of building a new type of coffee shop, Howard Schultz has paved his own path to success that you can surely follow.

"Expect more than others think possible."
– Howard Schultz

Chapter 4

Al – A Life Filled with Struggles

Born in 1879, Al did not speak until he was four years old. Most children start talking around 18 to 24 months, but Al could not speak until four. Being very slow with verbal development, his parents became concerned about his future fearing he would become a liability to society. To make matters worse, Al could not read until he was seven years old. To put that into perspective as well, most children are able to read around the age of five. These two vital skills took him much longer to learn than all other children of the same age.

As Al progressed through grade school, he encountered many struggles within the school walls due to his rebellious nature. One of his teachers described him as being "mentally slow, unsociable, and adrift forever in his foolish dreams." Not only did the school system have no faith in Al, but neither did his parents who also believed he was mentally handicapped and anti-social. Parents and teachers are critically important to the self-confidence of a young child, and the only belief Al could embrace about himself was that he was a complete failure.

At 16 years old in 1895, he was expelled from school by his teacher for the negative effects he had on his peers. Al had always desired to attend a university to continue his education at a higher level, but he now found himself expelled from high school. Even though his parents had given up on him and he was no longer even able to attend school, he still believed his dream was possible.

All Al knew up to this point in his life was failure. He had never tasted a drop of success, and his parents and the school system believed he would forever be a failure at everything he does. Despite the label society affixed on him, and the fact that he did not even have a high school diploma, he still attempted to enter the Federal Polytechnic School in Switzerland (similar to a top college in the U.S.) by sitting for its extremely difficult entrance exam. With his courage and inner belief that he would pass this examination and be accepted into this university, can you guess the outcome? Al failed the entrance exam and was denied admission into this esteemed educational institute.

When you are working towards an accomplishment or on an endeavor in your life and you fail at it, you can either look at all those hours spent as having added significant value to your being because you learned valuable lessons along the way and obtained knowledge that you would have otherwise never had the opportunity of learning, or you can view it as a waste of time. But why would a failure ever be considered a waste of time? Each failure brings with it the seed of an equivalent success because of the knowledge, experience, and principles that the failure has taught you.

Even though he failed the entrance exam, Al had done exceptionally well on the test in the areas of math and science. Realizing he needed to improve his knowledge in other academic fields, Al made the decision to continue his formal learning by enrolling in a new high school; thereafter, he would attempt that university's entrance exam again. After putting in over a year's worth of studying, Al was finally able to pass the entrance exam and achieve his goal of attending the Federal Polytechnic School. However, Al soon developed a horrible reputation within the university due to his poor behavior – he frequently skipped class and his fellow students and professors thought he was a joke with absolutely no potential. In his final year of study, no teacher would give him a recommendation when it came time to find a job. He was the only student out of his entire graduating class to have no research position offer upon graduation. It was at this hopeless time that Al wrote a letter apologizing to his parents wishing he was never born. His father died soon after, and thus his father only knew Al as an utter failure. Al let his failures consume him as he believed the negative opinions about himself from others, and he began to feel as though his life lost purpose.

While you are achieving your dreams, you must always remember the saying: "If there is no enemy within, the enemy outside can do us no harm." You have to be completely comfortable with who you are and what you are about. The opinions of others will become irrelevant when you respect yourself enough and have a purpose behind why you do what you do. Then, all of the negativity you hear will just simply be noise that has no impact on who you are or where your life is going.

After graduating college, Al had almost zero employment prospects, and he desperately struggled to find a job. He ended up working multiple low-paying jobs for a few years, but he yearned for something more permanent that would pay a better income. Due to his lack of employment credentials, it was a very difficult process for Al. He eventually ended up working in a patent office as a technical assistant examining invention applications. His passion always lied in the physics and mathematics field, but he was now employed in an entirely different profession. He became very discouraged doing work that had no real meaning to him other than a paycheck. Yet, this man who failed in school and remarkably disappointed his parents was still contemplating his dream of being a physicist, but up until this point in his life, the unrelenting failures were devouring his state of mind.

Allowing failure to consume you is a choice; you are personally making that decision. You can either let the failure immobilize you and create overwhelming fear, or you can make the decision to move on from those failures and continue to think positively. We as humans are programmed to think negatively, it is how we are biologically developed, and the world only reinforces this programming. The world loves to focus on the negative, which is why the news always covers negative events and people always talk about all the negatives in their lives instead of all the positives. What society fails to see is that failure should be embraced; it means you are trying something new. No one on this Earth was an expert the first time he did something. Every person who has ever achieved anything notable in his particular field faced failure over and over again on his way to success. Failure is an inevitable part of the process. If you try something new, you are going to indubitably fail and embarrass yourself. But you will not be like that forever if you continuously practice at your endeavor as you will soon gain the knowledge, skills, and experience needed to succeed.

Al worked incessantly at the patent office to allow extra time for his own research and studies outside of the office. A few years into his job, he began to publish his own independent work as a physicist. He published the "Special Theory of Relativity" in 1905 and submitted it to a scientific magazine, along with a few other research papers, and had great hope that he would hear back. Nevertheless, as the months passed with no response, Al became very saddened. His once high hopes that his theory would eventually make a profound effect on the scientific community came crashing down.

The path to success is not a smooth, flat road that you will travel down but rather a bumpy, windy road filled with potholes along the way. If the road was peaceful and easy to drive down, it would have many travelers – which is why this road to success is far less traveled. It requires a great amount of effort and persistence to navigate through all the hills, potholes, twists, and blind turns, but if you are passionate about what you do, you will find these obstacles as being nothing but a temporary inconvenience on your way to your destination.

It would not be long after these feelings of disappointment that Al would soon begin to draw attention from physicists for his previously submitted research. The "Special Theory of Relativity" and his other research papers from 1905 were ultimately published in one of the best known physicist journals at the time. Gaining a great deal of ambition and hunger from this recognition, Al decided to revisit his "Special Theory of Relativity" in 1907, which only applied to limited situations, and find a general theory of relativity that would apply in all instances (relating to the speed of light and space-time). This would require him to challenge his idol, Sir Isaac Newton – a legendary physicist in our society.

After demonstrating to the scientific community his numerous research studies that he had worked on over the years, he received an offer in 1908 to work at a top university in Germany that came with many perks. At this point, he was highly desired by all the universities and each was begging him to conduct his research at their location. Remember, this is the same Al who was expelled from school, failed his college entrance exam, and was thought to be a complete failure.

If Al had accepted his limited state of being to the multiple low-paying jobs he held in the early 1900's, he would have never reached these achievements he was always capable of. Instead, he woke up each morning with the goal of trying to become a better physicist than he was the day before. Just because you are temporarily at a bad point in your life does not mean that is how your life will always be. As long as you keep trying, you are not a failure. Success is simply trying one more time at something you failed at. If you decide to try out for that sports team one more time, or take that class one more time, or give your business another chance at succeeding, then you will be considered a success when it does succeed that next time around.

In 1911, while in the midst of working on his "Theory of General Relativity," Al received an invite to a conference for the best scientists in Europe. As the youngest professor in the group, he was identified as being one of the best talents emerging in the field of science. Al became an instant hit at the conference with everyone attracted to him for his intelligence, comedic personality, and friendly demeanor. Quite ironic that this is the same person whose parents and teachers thought he was mentally handicapped and anti-social.

While Al worked on his "Theory of General Relativity," he became very close with a fellow physicist by the name of Max Planck. Being a very intelligent physicist himself, Max told Al that he was not going to be successful with his relativity theory because the problem Al was studying was too hard and no one will ever believe him. This was told to Al by a highly respected physicist that was close friends with him, so why would Al not listen to him and save all that time he would "waste" trying? Because Al believed in himself and his capabilities despite the contrary.

Even when no one believes in your dream, you must listen to your own inner voice and continue on. If you are trying to accomplish a great feat, people will tell you that you are crazy, that it cannot be done, and that you are better off trying something more realistic. But it only takes you believing in yourself to make your dream happen, and Al begins to exhibit this.

After almost 10 years of ruthless research and studying, Al finalized his "Theory of General Relativity" in 1916. Think about this for a moment, Al spent almost 10 years on one theory! And you are trying to say you cannot graduate from college because it takes four years? Or that you cannot lose weight because it takes one year? Or that you cannot pass that exam because it takes one week of studying? Think again about all the excuses you give about endeavors that you say "take too much time to achieve."

Furthermore, in order for Al to prove that his "Theory of General Relativity" was accurate, he would need to photograph a solar eclipse, which is very infrequent in nature. After a failed attempt with his team to photograph a solar eclipse in June of 1918, Al would have to painfully wait almost a whole year until the next eclipse in May of 1919 to test his new theory again. The solar eclipse would take place between Chile and Peru in South America, and in the days leading up to the eclipse, the area was struck by heavy rain and clouds.

On the day of the eclipse, a tremendous storm hit that region, and Al feared that the weather would not allow for the proper photograph. However, just before the eclipse was to take place, the rain stopped and his team was able to get only one "quality" photo. This one photograph was enough evidence to prove that Al's "Theory of General Relativity" was true, and it shook the scientific world.

Even though Al achieved grand success from this theory that took him over 12 years to prove accurate, he continued to relentlessly spend his days researching and studying new theories. Because of his everlasting commitment to the physics field, Al received in 1921 the coveted Nobel Prize for his contributions to Theoretical Physics. But would Al become content and satisfied with this most prestigious award and his current accomplishments and not want more out of himself?

Al continued to pour his heart into his endeavors over the coming years, and in 1946, his famous theory, $E = mc^2$, stunned the world. This theory was initially created by Al in 1905 along with his "Special Theory of Relativity," but it took him over 40 more years to finalize the proof. In this long period of time, his proof had failed seven times – in 1905, 1906, 1907, 1914, 1934, and 1946. It was not until the eighth attempt that Al's proof was correct. What if he gave up on his theory after 40 years of unsuccessful attempts? This equation would have never been known to society.

The world knows this man as Albert Einstein – one of the most renowned physicists to ever live on this Earth. Can you believe his name "Einstein" is synonymous with genius? This boy who did not speak until he was four years old, did not learn to read until he was seven, expelled out of school for miserable behavior, and failed his college entrance exam is considered to be one of the most intelligent human beings of all time.

So why are you feeling like a failure just because someone told you that you were not good enough? No one determines your reality but you. Failure is nothing more than an obstacle on your path to success. And during the darkest of hours, always believe in yourself when others do not. If Albert Einstein did not believe in himself, the world would have never been blessed with his infamous laws that forever changed the world.

"We cannot solve our problems with the same thinking we used when we created them."
– Albert Einstein

Chapter 5

Mariah – Rejection, Racism, and Continuous Challenges

Mariah was born in Huntington, New York in 1970 to a mother of Irish descent who was an opera singer, and to a father who was African American and Venezuelan and worked as an engineer.

At the age of three, Mariah's parent divorced, which created a large separation in her family. Her older sister moved in with her father, while Mariah and her brother stayed with their mother. This divorce left Mariah distraught at a very young age and in a lot of pain. By the time she was four years old, a year after her parents' messy divorce, Mariah began to seek peace at night by sneaking a radio under her bed covers and resting quietly while listening to music. As time would pass, Mariah and her father became very distant and they soon stopped seeing or speaking to each other.

Due to her family's ethnicity mix as well as her own, Mariah struggled considerably with her peers in her community because of it. Some of the worst acts of hatred towards their family included their neighbors poisoning their dogs, setting their car afire, burning crosses on their front lawn, and even a bullet shot through their window during dinner time. As well, Mariah was once spit on by a person in an attack of racism.

Childhood and adolescent years are difficult enough for children due to all the normal issues that arise during this period of time, and now imagine the stress and anxiety Mariah felt on top of this from being tormented over her race. She was viewed as a complete outcast in her neighborhood, and it was difficult for her to be accepted. Not only that, but her actual safety was at risk. Their family car was blown up in flames – all that hard-earned money they spent on it was now completely gone with a useless, burned car. Fortunately, no one in her family was in that car at the time it was set afire. In addition, someone shot a bullet through the window in their home during dinner time, but fortunately again, no one was injured by it. Living in a state of fear, Mariah had far more to worry about than trying to follow the latest fashion trend in school. We are all members of the human race; and ethnicity, religion, gender, or any other form of identification have nothing to do with the potential of an individual – people should be evaluated based on their own internal character.

Mariah's life only became more challenging as her single mother struggled to provide Mariah and her brother with the basic necessities of life as they fought against poverty. As a result of her living conditions, Mariah began to develop insecurities about herself at school. After her mother enslaved herself in work for several years, she was able to move them all into a better area of New York as the area of town they had previously lived in was a very poor and crime-ridden neighborhood.

While people remember and value monumental successes in their life, it is their triumphs over the difficult challenges that truly add the most value. Think back to a time in your life when you were faced with a problematic opportunity (because everything in our lives that happens has hidden opportunity inside of it), and then think about that feeling you had when you overcame it. It brings great joy in knowing that we did not fall down to the challenges but rather rose above them. It is getting through the surprise punches life throws, the obstacles you face, and the stumbles on your ascent that will truly give you the most self-confidence in knowing what you are capable of and what you can fight through.

While attending high school, Mariah found that her interests lied in only a few subjects; these were music, art, and literature. Finding where her passion was, Mariah began to write poems in her teenage years and added melodies to them – basically creating mini-songs. With her mother being an opera singer, Mariah began to work on her usage of the whistle register with her mother, which is the highest register of the human voice. It is very difficult to master the whistle register as it requires relentless and enduring training to have the ability to control it, but Mariah knew she was capable of doing it.

In high school, Mariah crossed paths with a friend named Gavin whom she discovered also had a passion for the music industry. She began to write songs with Gavin, which is an unremitting process due to the amount of creativity and originality that writing songs requires. They composed their first duet together in her senior year of high school, and it took a significant toll on the young Maria. She would travel into New York City to write songs with Gavin as soon as the school day ended, and she would not return back to her house until around 3am, where she would shortly have to wake up at 7am for school again. Gavin would eventually move onto other things soon after, but Mariah energetically continued writing songs. Shortly after graduating high school in 1987, Mariah moved to Manhattan to live in a one-bedroom apartment, which she shared with four other female students in order to be able to afford the cost of rent.

In your pursuit of your goals, if you do what is easy, your life will be hard – but if you do what is hard, your life will be easy. It would have been much easier for Mariah to stay with her mother writing songs at home than to take the risk to move to Manhattan, live with four complete strangers, and press herself financially to afford rent. Let's say your goal is to lose weight and have better health, it is very easy to continue with your "comfortable" lifestyle that got you to the position you are currently in of being overweight, but if you decide to continue like this, your life will continue to be hard having to deal with all the repercussions that come from being overweight such as major health issues and a lack of self-confidence. Yet if you decide to do what is "hard," which is to lose weight by exercising regularly and making smart choices with the food you put into your body, then you will lose weight, your health and self-confidence will improve tremendously, and your life will be much easier. When faced with the decision of doing what is easy or what is hard, always make the decision to do what is hard because you know what the end result will be – a much easier and happier life.

With no college education, no prior resources from her single mother or alienated father, and a rent bill that was due every month along with all the other financial obligations that came with supporting herself, Mariah began working as a waitress and a coat check girl at several restaurants. However, Mariah failed miserably at these basic jobs and was usually fired after only two weeks. She would consistently mess up orders and she was rude to the customers. As a result, she would often not receive a tip, which is a direct reflection on the quality of service she provided the paying and deserving customer. During her breaks at both jobs, Mariah would use her break time to scribble down lyrics that would pop in and out of her head during her hours she was serving customers.

Your results in life are going to reflect how committed you are to your endeavor. It is evident that Mariah lacked the passion for her day jobs of being a waitress and coat check girl as she did not put forth any commitment into providing the customers with her best service. Due to this, her results, which are the tips she received, reflected her level of commitment. Do not expect your results to change if you do not change your level of commitment towards your endeavor. You need to be fully committed to your dream if you want to begin to see real progress. Take the example mentioned above with the individual trying to lose weight. If he is only partially committed to losing weight, let's say he goes to the gym maybe once a week and only occasionally focuses on eating the proper foods, he will receive partial results because his results are directly correlated to his partial commitment. If he decides to become fully committed, he will exercise daily and ensure each meal contains the proper nutrients, and this level of commitment will reflect his much quicker and better results as his results will reflect that of someone who is fully committed.

While being fired often from her day jobs, Mariah worked doggedly at night on her musical ambitions. After spending many hours over countless, tiresome nights, she was finally able to finish her demo tape that consisted of only four songs. Since she lived in Manhattan, she had all the record label companies in the vicinity, and Mariah took the initiative of delivering her demo tapes personally to these conglomerates. Upon entrance into all of these different companies, Mariah could never get past the front desk to someone of higher standing at the record label. She was forced to leave her demo tapes with the company's receptionist who would promise to give it to the right person internally. With the courage to approach all of these large companies, can you guess what her outcome was? Every record label either rejected her or she heard no response back from them.

Instead of making excuses, Mariah continued to ignore the failures and accepted them for what they were, knowing in the end, it would be these record label companies who would miss out on the opportunity to sign her. In life, no one will care about your excuses, they hold absolutely no meaning. People use excuses to try and justify their inaction or inability to achieve the results they wanted because they did not want to make sacrifices and put in the time, effort, and pain that would be needed in order to achieve success. The only people that may even remotely care about your excuses are your family members, and many times they will not care about the reasons why you failed to achieve something either. No one in this world will care about your excuses on why you did not achieve something; it is your results that are the only thing that matters. If you want to apply for that scholarship and you need a certain GPA, will the scholarship committee care that you had to work a job while attending classes and that is why you were not able to maintain your GPA level? Or will your coach care that your relationship ended with your significant other and you allowed it to ruin your performance on the field which cost your team the championship game? When you see the score of a basketball game, is there a little asterisk next to the score of the losing team saying two of the players were overcoming injuries during the game which was the team's excuse for losing? No – the only thing shown is the final result of the game.

While in Manhattan, her childhood insecurities and her stage fright intensified. The best way to fight back against fear is to do the exact thing you are of afraid of doing, and so Mariah began to conquer her stage fright by performing live on stage in New York City on a very small scale. One night after she sang miserably, she was waiting outside the building of the place she had just performed at, and she began speaking to a drummer who also just had his performance. They instantly began to relate well to each other, and by the end of their conversation, the drummer had agreed to introduce her to a rising star in the industry by the name of Brenda.

In December 1988, Mariah attended an executive's gala with Brenda where a man by the name of Tommy, who was the head of Columbia Records (one of the largest record label companies), was in attendance. Even though she had no popularity yet, Mariah took the courage of going up to Tommy and handing him her demo tape. When Tommy left the party and began his drive home, he started listening to her demo tape in the car. After only two songs, Tommy was so enamored by her talented voice that he instantly turned around to go back to the party to see if Mariah was still in attendance; however, she had just left. After two weeks of searching for Mariah, Tommy was finally able to get in contact with her and they finalized her deal with his company, Columbia Records.

Instead of celebrating that she finally made it into one of the largest record label companies, Mariah worked harder than ever before on her music. Mariah released her self-titled debut album in 1990, and despite Columbia Records promoting her as their main female artist, she had very low sales upon the initial release of her debut album. However, her album not only gained popularity over the next year, but it became an absolute sensation. Her debut album went multiplatinum, and in 1991, it was the best-selling album throughout the entire United States.

Just because you are not seeing the results you want now does not mean they are not going to come. Mariah and Columbia Records did not see the success they wanted with her self-titled debut album upon its initial release, but because they continued to believe in the content they created, her album eventually hit the top of the charts the following year. If you are trying to start up a business and you focus on selling quality products but you have not had the sales you want initially, continue with it and your success will come if you do not give up on it. If you are trying to become a better parent to change your child's behavior, do not give up because you have not seen much change yet – continue to work on your methods and continue to lead by example. Soon enough, you will see small change after small change in your child, and eventually, these tiny changes will culminate into an entirely new lifestyle for him.

After her 1990 debut album, Mariah released another album the following year in 1991 which was criticized by many for being of a lower quality than her previous album; however, she ignored the opinions of her critics and sold over 8,000,000 copies. Her critics would continue their attempt to find her weaknesses and speculation grew that Mariah was a "studio worm" incapable of reaching her 5-octave vocal range and perfect pitch she was known for outside of the studio (basically claiming that the studio had altered and manufactured her voice in her songs to sound better than she really was). Devising the best way to silence her critics and demonstrate her astonishing singing skills that she worked so arduously on, she appeared on an episode of MTV where she sang the cover version of "I'll Be There" by the Jackson Five as well as six other new songs. This episode on MTV received such vast attention that the company, Sony, decided to release these hits as an EP, otherwise known as extended play, (because there were not enough songs to qualify as an album), and it was given triple Platinum certification as well as Gold and Platinum Certifications across Europe.

If Mariah did not have critics and haters doubting her abilities, she would have never been presented with this drive to find an opportunity to prove them wrong – which only resulted in greater success for her. The critics in your life are going to try to take you down because you are achieving something they wish they could achieve, and while it may be difficult to hear insults they spew out, they will provide you with opportunities to succeed in ways you never would have had without them.

In 1993, Mariah would marry Tommy (from Columbia Records) and she would release another album that year, which despite the mixed reviews again from critics, became one of the bestselling albums of all-time. It seemed like all was going perfectly with her successful career and now happy marriage.

However, like Mariah had known all too well in her life, she was about to face tenacious challenges once again over the next few years that could have easily destroyed her career had she let them. Her older sister received horrid news that she had contracted AIDS, and Mariah had to learn to cope and accept this disease her sister would now be living with. Feeling great pain over her sister, Mariah transferred this pain into her creative work in the studio and wrote the song "One Sweet Day," which when released as a single on her next album in 1995, became the longest running number-one song in United States history. She used her pain to push her to greatness, and it allowed her to achieve something that she may never have produced had she not gone through that pain.

While you are in the quest of achieving your dreams, you are going to experience pain in some type of way. When you do experience this pain, you can either let it internally consume you and overtake your being, or you can transfer it out and put it into what you are externally doing. Just like Mariah, if you transfer your pain into your endeavor, you will see results you have never seen before because that pain will push you to think in ways you never thought before, do things you never thought about trying, and take calculated risks you were too afraid of taking.

In 1998, Mariah and her husband Tommy divorced due to numerous issues they were facing between their personal and business lives. Since Tommy was the head of Columbia Records, Mariah faced problems at the company and ultimately left in 2000 where she signed a $100M recording contract with Virgin Records America.

The obstacles would only keep coming for Mariah, as in July 2001, she suffered a physical and emotional breakdown and was hospitalized for severe exhaustion. It was during this time that she was starring in the movie, *Glitter*, which had an accompanying sound track as well. Along with all the time spent preparing, acting, and singing for the movie, Mariah also had to do interviews all day long – she would get only two hours of sleep per night, if even that much.

Mariah remained under doctor's care for two weeks, and the film *Glitter*, due to the media attention surrounding her state of being, was unsuccessful. Her sound track for the movie became her lowest selling album to date, and as a result, she was bought out of her contract with Virgin Records America by Island Records for $50M (half of her previous contract) – and her career began to decline. If things could not get any worse for Mariah, later this same year in 2001, her father, who she had barely spoken to since childhood, died of cancer.

Just like music had been soothing to her when her parents divorced as a child, Mariah immersed herself in the studio and transferred all of this pain yet again into working on her next album. In 2004, even though many critics defined her career as being officially over, she released her 10th album which went right to the top of the music charts, and one of the songs in the album remained #1 on the U.S charts for 14 weeks, an unbelievable feat for even the greatest of musicians. While she could have wisely ended her career coming off this remarkable 10th album, she continued to release new albums over the next decade that saw an abundance of success.

This female artist, known as Mariah Carey, still continues to pursue her passion to this day. In her remarkable career so far, she has won five Grammy Awards, 11 American Music Awards, 14 Billboard Music Awards, and 19 World Music Awards. Mariah Carey was named the world's best-selling recording artist of the

1990's, her song "We Belong Together" was named by Billboard as the "Song of the Decade," and she has spent a total of 79 weeks at the #1 position on the Billboard Hot 100, which is the greatest number of weeks by any artist in United States history. After struggling financially for so many years, Mariah is now one of the wealthiest female artists in history with a net worth of over $500M. Mariah Carey has established herself as one of the top 10 best-selling artists of all-time, and due to her unique vocal style and singing ability which had been rejected over and over again by record label companies, Mariah Carey has left a legacy that will forever impact the music industry.

"If you just see me as the princess, then you misunderstand who I am and what I have been through."
– Mariah Carey

Chapter 6

Les – Educable Mentally Retarded

In 1945, Les was born on an abandoned floor in a building in Miami, Florida in a part of town struck by poverty known as "Liberty City." Les and his twin brother, Wesley, were born to a woman who became pregnant from another man while her husband was away at war. His biological mother did not want her husband knowing about her unfaithful act or these two "mistake" children, so she decided to give Les and his brother away to a random stranger when they were six weeks old. She told their adoptive mother to never tell either of them about their real mother. His adoptive mother was Mamie, a 38-year-old, single woman who had no children of her own, very little education (up to only a third grade level), and in a current situation of severe poverty. She adopted Les and his brother with absolutely no idea how to raise them, or even the resources to do so. Mamie worked in a school cafeteria earning minimum wage, and Les grew up without a father or ever knowing his real mother.

In the fifth grade, the education system labeled Les as being "educable mentally retarded" because of his inability to stop talking and his poor grades in school. As a result of this label, the school placed him in a special education class and moved him back to the fourth grade. "Educable mentally retarded" is defined as someone who is mildly impaired in both their intellectual learning and adaptive behavior. As an adult, the person will have a mental age between 8 and 12 years old and will be limited to learning basic academic subjects up to only a sixth grade level.

While in grade school, Les had failed both the fifth and eighth grade and frequently had to attend summer school. He viewed himself as a failure and being someone who lacked any talents or abilities, and the school system only reinforced his negative belief. Failing twice before he even entered high school and being labeled as very mentally slow, Les developed serious self-esteem issues and began to embrace the label placed on him of being "educable mentally retarded."

It took significant, repetitive encouragement from his mother and one special teacher in high school to help him see himself beyond the limiting and destructive label of "educable mentally retarded." These two positive influences in his life helped him realize his potential, which he had a tremendous amount within him waiting to be discovered; but he could not see it at a young age nor could the school system due to his energetic nature. Instead of trying to work with Les on cultivating his dynamic personality and overcoming his lack of self-confidence, the school system thought it would be much easier to falsely label him as being mentally inept for school.

Disregard any negative opinion that others have of you. Embrace only the positive opinions you hear, and most importantly, maintain your confidence that you do possess attributes that others wish they had. No one in this world is perfect. There are many individuals that you look up to that wish they had an attribute you possess, whether it be your intelligence, athletic ability, patience, ability to listen and understand, your ability to convince others, or any other attribute. Everybody on this Earth wishes they had a certain attribute, so begin to see how powerful you actually are because of the attributes you possess that others wish they had.

Ever since he was adopted, Les was always inspired by his adoptive mother because of all that she did for him considering his real mother gave him away to a complete stranger without any concern for his well-being. Even though Les never knew his maternal mother, and grew up without a father in the midst of extreme poverty, he always promised his adoptive mother he would one day buy her a home. He formed an inseparable bond to his adoptive mother and dreamed of having the opportunity to provide for her someday like she did for him with the little resources she had. However, judging by Les' atrocious performance in school, it seemed far from reality that he would ever have the ability to purchase a home for his mother, let alone his own eventual family.

Along with his mother, the one special teacher that forever changed his life was LeRoy Washington. LeRoy was a speech and drama instructor at Booker T. Washington High School in Miami, FL. One day as a junior in high school, he listened to Mr. Washington give a speech to the soon-to-be graduating senior class. He snuck into the back of the auditorium, even though he was not supposed to, and listened to this speech that would forever change his life. Mr. Washington told all these graduating students that their dreams were "possible."

One day at school, Les was waiting for his friend who was in the classroom of the influential teacher, Mr. Leroy Washington. While patiently waiting for his friend, Mr. Washington asked Les to write something on the board for him, and Les replied that since he was not one of his students, he could not do that. After

Mr. Washington replied back that it did not matter and to follow his directions now, Les said that he could not do that because he was educable mentally retarded. Mr. Washington fiercely stood up from behind his desk and said "Do not ever say that again. Someone's opinion of you does not have to become your reality."

Les had a very negative view of himself, and Mr. Washington helped Les change that mindset and begin to see his own potential. Les would tell himself over and over again those powerful words Mr. Washington told him that day, which were "someone's opinion of you does not have to become your reality." Being someone that loved to talk to people, Les would imagine himself speaking to thousands, and he would even write on pieces of paper "I am the world's greatest orator."

The belief we have about ourselves will be reflected in what we do and how we act. The process of writing down a positive affirmation about yourself will cause your mind to actually embrace and act as if you really possess that affirmation. The same is true when faced with a difficult, momentary situation. Let's say you are running a timed mile around the track, and half way through, the lactic acid begins to fill your legs, your muscles begin to feel the burning rubber below your feet, and your mind as a result begins to weaken. If during your run, you tell yourself a positive affirmation over and over such as "I am full of energy and I feel great," your body will actually embody this belief as the truth.

By telling Les his dreams were possible, Mr. Washington planted seeds in Les' mind that shifted his inner belief. Les believed up to that point in his life that he was a failure because he had failed twice in school and was labeled "educable mentally retarded" by the school system. But Mr. Washington helped Les realize the vast amount of potential he had within him that was waiting to be unlocked and exposed for all of the world to see.

Writing down your goal helps remind you why you are willing to endure the pain and sacrifice necessary to achieve it.

When difficult times confront you in your pursuit, you can look back at your written goal to remember and recreate that feeling of excitement you had at that moment when you initially wrote it down. I want you to take the time now to write down your goal on a piece of paper and put it away in your wallet or purse. The next time a difficult situation arises and you face a cemented brick wall in front of your dream, pull out the slip of paper with your written goal and relive those jubilant feelings. This will help refresh you on the why behind what you are doing so that you do not lose focus on what you set out to achieve. With every wall we face on our path to success, we can either figure out a solution to get past it, or we can allow it to thwart us and turn us around. Some walls will be harder to get through then others, but with enough hits, the brick wall will crumble and you will proceed on your journey.

You must also always believe in yourself, even when others tell you it will never happen. In defiance of the label placed on him by the school system of being "educable mentally retarded," Les envisioned himself speaking to thousands of people onstage as the world's best orator. You must believe in yourself at all times, because if you do not, who will?

In a situation where an important task needs to be performed and the instructor has the option of choosing between a self-confident individual and an individual without any self-confidence (all else being held equal), the instructor will always choose the self-confident individual. Confidence is one of the greatest strengths in life and it is one of the most visible attributes to others that a person possesses.

After finally graduating high school, Les worked as a city sanitation worker. Once again, he felt as though he was in a position where others looked down upon him. Even though he was now years into his life and at a juncture where many would consider him past the point of having the ability to change his circumstances, he continued to believe that one day he would be able to pursue his dream of radio broadcasting. Not satisfied with the path his life was walking down, Les decided to take action.

Without having any credentials, Les decided to take the risk of walking into the office of a radio station inquiring for a job. The owner asked him if he had any experience as a broadcaster, and Les politely replied "No sir, I don't." The owner then asked him if he had any experience in journalism, which Les also responded "No sir, I don't." Lacking the qualifications, the owner promptly told Les there were no jobs available. Despite the disappointing rejection, Les continued to walk into that local radio station office each day asking if there were any new jobs available. Even though he kept hearing that same response, Les continued to ask until one day, the owner hired him. The only reason he was hired after continuous rejections was because of his willingness to keep trying until he succeeded. While Les was able to finally be employed at this radio station, he was forced to do various odd, monotonous jobs – basically he did everything except what he really wanted to do which was radio broadcasting.

Instead of viewing these "chores" as being useless and a waste of his time, Les chose to see the hidden opportunity within them. If he could not be entrusted with perfecting these small tasks, then why would he ever be entrusted with a large, important, and meaningful task? Despite seeing no signs of change or progress around him, he remained focused on trying to become the best worker at these small tasks the office had ever seen. He knew that it was preparing him for the day where his moment to demonstrate his speaking ability would come.

If you keep working at what you want and remain persistent, your opportunity will eventually present itself. But you must ensure that you will be prepared for that opportunity by practicing your craft as if you have already been in that elusive position for years. It is worse to be presented with an opportunity and not be ready for it, then it is to have never been presented with the opportunity at all.

A "lucky" opportunity did finally present itself to Les one day. He had a chance to shine when the current radio jockey was removed for being drunk on air, and Les was the only other person at the station who could possibly fill in for him. Sometimes in life we get that one break, that one moment, where our fate rests in us seizing the opportunity given, and the deciding factor on whether it will positively or negatively change our destiny forever lies in our preparation for that moment.

Les took full advantage of this one opportunity and managed to impress the owner enough that he let him be on air full time. If Les had told himself he was only going to rehearse his speaking when he was first given the opportunity to be on air, Les would have been ill-prepared for this destiny-changing moment; and who knows when the next similar opportunity would have occurred, if at all.

We are all given an opportunity in life. Regardless of whether you think it was an opportunity or not, we have all been given chances to succeed, and it is solely up to us to be ready. Yes, you have had opportunities in your life. I know you are thinking that you never had the opportunity to play in a game this season to show your coach your abilities, or you never had the opportunity to show your boss why you should be promoted, but there were countless opportunities that you did not identify as being an opportunity. As an athlete, you have the opportunity to impress your coach every day in practice, but you choose to only see the opportunity as having the chance to play in a game. The opportunity lies in the practice each day, not in the game that week. As an employee, your opportunity to show your boss why you have earned a promotion is through all the little things you do every day. It is not this one large project or task asked of you that will determine your promotion, but the continual ability to perform well in both the small and large tasks asked of you. As a student, your opportunity to do well is in every homework assignment you complete; not that test at the end of the curriculum. If you treat every homework assignment like it is the final test, you will ace that exam when it is given to you. This is true for all professions in life.

After his gig in the radio business, Les wanted to pursue his life goal of becoming a motivational speaker. He took the risk of moving to Detroit from Florida with nothing but clothes and one recorded tape of his motivational speeches.

How many of you would take that risk? Move to an entirely different part of the country with absolutely no resources, all to take the risk of achieving your dreams. In Detroit, he rented an office which he shared with an attorney, where he worked day and night to achieve this dream of his. Les would begin his workday before sun rise and would still be grinding away well past sun down. He slept on the cold, hard office floor because he did not have the money to live in an apartment and was forced to bathe in the bathroom sink. He poured every ounce of his soul into this endeavor of becoming a motivational speaker.

Now think about this, a man who was told he was "educable mentally retarded" and failed numerous times in school believes he can be a motivational speaker, quite ironic right? If Les had the confidence in himself to pursue his dreams, then there is no reason you should ever not believe in yourself. He read a myriad of books on public speaking and studied the habits of successful speakers to understand what made them successful. In your profession, you need to study the habits of the leaders in your field and understand what makes them different from you. Is it they work longer hours, accept tasks others view as being insignificant, or read more books to further their knowledge on the particular field? Whatever it is, you need to do it, and Les understood this.

In this office building in Detroit, Les wrote on the mirror in the bathroom, "I can make it." Even though he was sleeping on the office building floor and bathing in the bathroom sink, he still believed his dream was possible. People in the office laughed when they saw him as he was the foolish man believing in his senseless dreams, but Les repeated this line "I can make it" over and over to himself to the point where his mind believed this as being his current state of reality.

Were there times when Les wanted to quit? It was actually quite often that he felt the overpowering feeling of self-pity and despair when it seemed his dreams would not be possible. But Les developed the habit of learning to immediately replace negative thoughts with self-reassuring thoughts of "I can make it" and "it's possible." Our minds will be overtaken by negative thoughts if we do not feed positive thoughts into our mind. Think of your mind as having two lions in it that are constantly fighting. The first lion is considered to be the "bad lion" that feeds on negativity, self-pity, despair, and anything else that is evil. The other lion is the "good lion" that feeds on positivity, self-confidence, possibilities, and hope. These two lions are constantly fighting each other, and so you may ask, who wins the fight? The lion that wins is whichever one you feed.

Les was able to finally get a gig speaking to elementary students, then high school students, and eventually companies. After four years of speaking to students and companies, he received the highest award given by the National Speakers Association, and Fortune 500 companies would be anxiously requesting him to come speak at their corporations at a rate of over $25,000 per hour. In 1998, Les was earning more than $4.5 million dollars per year from his public speaking engagements and appearances on T.V.

This man, known as Les Brown, accomplished the unimaginable feat of becoming one of the top motivational speakers in the world. He has positively changed the lives of millions of people, and many of his famous speeches have been posted to YouTube to inspire others for years to come (I recommend you listen to them).

Life is not only about growing as an individual, but also helping others live out their dreams.

Les overcame all of his insecurities and doubts, and he succeeded in reaching his life's dream. He would eventually purchase a multi-million dollar home for his mother in Florida to fulfill her dream of wanting her own home, just like he had promised when he was a young boy.

"You must be willing to do the things today others won't do in order to have the things tomorrow others won't have."

– Les Brown

Chapter 7

Abraham – Debt, Unpopularity, and Public Disapproval

A braham was born in 1809 in a one-room cottage in Kentucky. He had two siblings; however, his brother unfortunately died in infancy. Leaving only his sister, Abraham grew up typical of this era by helping his father provide for the family.

Having a close relationship to his mother, Abraham faced a serious setback early in his life when at the age of nine years old, his mother died – leaving his sister in charge of the house. The death of his mother had a crippling effect on Abraham, and it resulted in a further strain on his relationship with his father. Viewing his father as lazy and lacking ambition, Abraham developed an unfortunate resentment towards him at an early age, which only worsened during this tragic time. It was his negative view on his father's work ethic that created his inner desire to achieve more in life through hard work.

Although he had a tall, lean body that seemed like the perfect fit for physical labor, Abraham preferred reading and writing.

His neighbors and family would often criticize him for being lazy believing that he was just simply trying to avoid manual labor. However, Abraham understood the importance of knowledge and learning, and even though his parents were illiterate, he made the decision not to follow their paths, but rather to create his own trail.

While Abraham had only one year of combined formal education by a few teachers, he took it upon himself to learn more through self-education. Abraham gave himself an education through continuously reading books and writing. He would maintain a lifelong interest in learning.

In pursuit of your dreams, you may need to carve out your own trail like Abraham did and not follow society's path. Because if you follow that already traveled path, you will achieve the same results as every other person who traveled that way. Society's path is not always the best path to take, but many choose to take it because it is laid out in front of them and it is the easiest way to travel. They do not want to fight through the forestry and insects that lay ahead in creating their own trail, but would rather choose the effortless option of following others. If you do what others do, you will only get what they got. Most people will aim to do the least amount of work for the most benefit if possible. If you want to be somebody others look up to and follow, you need to lay your own trail that is properly created through ethical values and determination – and others will travel behind you in your now chartered footsteps.

In his later teenage years, Abraham became known for his skill in wielding an axe, so for a while he used this ability to make a living by splitting firewood. After moving to a small community within Illinois, Abraham took on a series of various jobs over the next few years which included being a shopkeeper and postmaster. While these may not have appeared to be the best opportunities for him, Abraham used them to acquire social skills as well as the ability to tell captivating stories, which would be invaluable to him later in life.

If you are not happy with where you are currently, instead of complaining about your temporary situation, think about all the skills and lessons you will walk away with when you leave it. Regardless of how uninterested you are or how minor your role may seem, this situation will provide you with assets that can be used later in life. For example, if your job is taking out the trash at a restaurant, among the many assets you will gain from this include consistency – for you always take out the garbage when it is full, organization – you properly dispose of the trash and keep the restaurant clean, dependency – the other employees and owners rely on you for doing your job, and amicability – always having a smile on your face and being someone others enjoy to be around. There are positives in any and every situation; it is all in how you look at it.

Now at 23 years old in 1832, Abraham made the decision to purchase a small general store in Illinois with a business partner on credit as he did not have the money to acquire it. The economy was booming in this region of Illinois, and it seemed to be a lucrative opportunity for him. Despite all the success in the surrounding area, Abraham's business seriously struggled. With an increasing amount of debt, Abraham sold off his share in the general store, but unfortunately, his business partner passed away with his debt still being outstanding.

Without the established modern day bankruptcy laws that provide much more protection to citizens, Abraham became liable for the $1,000 (around $25,000 adjusted to today's value) that his business partner owed in debt because they were initially in the business together. The creditors who had loaned the $1,000 to his now deceased business partner took Abraham to court, where he was found liable to pay for the remaining balance. To help pay off some of the liability, Abraham had to sell his two remaining assets which were his horse and some equipment. Since that was not enough to cover the entire amount of the liability, Abraham was forced to pay off the rest of the debt as he earned money, and it ended up taking him over 17 years to finally pay it off.

Imagine having this burden of debt on your shoulders for over 17 years, and it was not even his debt but that of his deceased business partner. Instead of succumbing to this challenging circumstance, he chose to overcome it. If you persist long enough, that obstacle in front of you will soon be behind you.

Later the same year that his business went bankrupt, Abraham went to serve in the Illinois Militia in the Black Hawk War, though he never saw any combat. While he was initially promoted to captain in his ranks, he would leave the service only a few months later after having been demoted to a private – a much lower rank in the military. How many of you would allow a demotion like this to permanently damage your self-esteem? Abraham did not let this demotion define his capabilities, and he continued carving his own trail when he returned home.

After returning from the war, Abraham began his political campaign running for the Illinois General Assembly. Without any previous experience in politics, he took a leap of faith by believing in his own abilities. Despite being a popular candidate and possessing great enthusiasm for politics, he lost the election.

Do not be discouraged just because the first time you do something you fail – that will occur more often than not. The only way to be successful at something is through practice and gaining the needed experience, so of course your first attempt will not produce the outcome you are looking for. But if you never try in the first place, then you will never take the first step towards being successful at it. Success is nothing but many little things collected together over time to form a large accomplishment. Without the small things done properly like each connected piece in a giant jigsaw puzzle, that grand success – like the overall image of the completed puzzle, will never be achieved.

Around the same time as the election for the Illinois General Assembly, Abraham developed a close relationship with a woman named Ann. He called her his first true love, and his heart was entrusted within her. Unfortunately, Ann passed away due to typhoid in 1835. This left Abraham very depressed, and still feeling the agony a year later in 1836, he suffered a nervous breakdown at the young age of 27 years old.

Despite his poor state of being, Abraham began to teach himself law by reading books on the subject. Without any instructor or friends to help him study, he took the initiative entirely upon himself to learn what people view as a complex subject. Through his incessant obsession with learning, Abraham was able to teach himself law, and in the same year as his nervous breakdown, he received permission by Illinois to practice law.

In life, people tend to quit right before they are about to see results. This is because it is at this moment where their obstacles seem too impossible to overcome and the negative reality that the world feeds on consumes their limitless minds. It is in the darkest hour of night that the sun begins to rise. As long as you continue working towards your dream, regardless of how small the steps may be, you will avoid the lasting pain of quitting that will haunt you for eternity. Like Abraham proves, the more you have been through, the more you can get through.

Abraham began to practice law and later worked with a fellow lawyer named John from 1841 to 1844. Just as Abraham was becoming friendly with John, he wrote John a letter saying "I am the most miserable man living. If what I feel were equally distributed to the whole human family, there would not be one cheerful face on the earth." As you can see, he became very negative and pessimistic about his past and the lack of potential he saw in his future.

Regardless of how badly you have failed, you are greater than your circumstances. If you run from your problems now, you will always run. Life is nothing more than habits, so if you develop the habit of running whenever you face a difficult moment in your life, you will turn that into a habit and you will always run.

Deciding to give his political career another chance, Abraham ran for speaker in the Illinois House of Representatives in 1838, and you know what the outcome was? He was defeated yet again and did not get elected. Despite now having failed to be elected twice, Abraham mustered up the courage to run for the House of Representatives again, and in 1846, he finally succeeded and was elected.

He would only end up serving one two-year term after failing to be re-elected for his position in 1848. When the presidential election swung around in 1849, Abraham ran for the Commissioner of the General Land Office, but he failed to be elected yet again.

Besides his one two-year term in the House of Representatives, Abraham had failed four times on a very large scale in his political career. While these failures were occurring, Abraham had four children with his wife in the 1840's and 1850's, and sadly three of their four children died –at the ages of 4, 12, and 18 years old. The death of his children had a profound effect on him, and as a result, Abraham suffered from clinical depression.

After his last failed attempt in the political arena to become Commissioner of the General Land Office, Abraham decided to return to practicing law where he began to develop an excellent reputation for himself, especially from a criminal trial where he got his plaintiff acquitted of charges by using a fact established by judicial notice to challenge the credibility of an eyewitness.

It would only be a matter of time until his passion for politics emerged again, and it occurred with passing of the Kansas-Nebraska Act in 1852. This act gave individual states the ability to decide whether to allow slavery, and Abraham with his fierce opposition to slavery, had his political zeal awakened within him. He made the decision to run for Vice President in 1856, but as Abraham had known failure all too well, his attempt to run for this coveted position in the United States (voted for at his party's National Convention) failed as he came in second. He then ran for Senate against Stephen Douglas, which is still considered to be one of the most publicized debates of all time. After hours of preparation and seven grueling rounds of intense debates, Abraham failed yet again and lost another election.

No one will care how much you prepared for an endeavor or how large your desire to succeed was – you will only be judged on your results. Second place is never remembered, and might as well be the same as last place because both are completely forgotten. Do you remember who received the silver medal in an Olympic event, or who was in second place in terms of being your school's valedictorian? What about the person who was next in line to be considered to help write the Constitution as one of the founding fathers? History only remembers first place.

Despite seeing nothing but failure in his political career, Abraham continued on and decided to run for the highest position possible in the United States – the presidency. Advocating against slavery, Abraham only won two of the 996 voting counties in all the Southern (Confederate) states. Regardless of that fact that his views on abolishing slavery would create fierce opposition in the South, Abraham demanded change for what he believed was right. In 1861, the 16th President of the United States was declared, and his name was Abraham Lincoln.

During his tenure from 1861 up to his assassination in 1865, Abraham Lincoln led the United States through the Civil War, and in the process of doing so, he abolished slavery, modernized the economy, and strengthened the federal government. His famous Emancipation Proclamation executive order, along with his passing of the Thirteenth Amendment to the Constitution, permanently outlawed slavery in the United States. By many scholars, Abraham Lincoln is considered to be the best President the United States has ever had. His face is on the U.S. five dollar bill as well as the one cent penny. The capital of Nebraska has been named after him in his honor as well as numerous other cities and towns across the country. The Lincoln Memorial, one of the most visited monuments in Washington, DC, as well as the sculpture of his face on Mount Rushmore, were tributes to Abraham Lincoln for all of his successful endeavors in life that were born out of many failures.

"We can complain because rose bushes have thorns,
or rejoice because thorn bushes have roses."
– Abraham Lincoln

Chapter 8

Mike – Lack of Skill and Cut from the Team

B orn in 1963 in Brooklyn, New York, Mike was an average boy to say the least. He was not famous or well-known, did not have any special qualities, and he was not born into a "privileged" family. As a young child, his family moved from New York to Wilmington, North Carolina, where he would spend his childhood years. Mike was what many people would call a "typical kid" – he enjoyed recreational sports but could sometimes be quite lazy when playing. He always knew what he wanted, but it would take a personal tragedy to ignite the flame within him to unlock his inner potential.

As a sophomore in high school, he tried out for his high school varsity basketball team. Standing at 5'11", Mike thought he had practiced enough beforehand to make the team and that he possessed the skills necessary to be on it. Following the tryout, Mike did not see his name posted on the final roster – he was cut from the varsity team. His coach told him he was too short to play basketball and not skilled enough to play at a varsity level, but instead should play on the JV (junior varsity) team. Following this news, he locked himself in his room and cried. Basketball was more than a sport to Mike, it was his passion. But now, his dream of becoming a professional basketball player seemed impossible. He felt hopeless and had a loss of meaning in his life.

To be a professional, you have to be the best in the world. If Mike could not even make his high school team, where he was competing against only a handful of other individuals within his town, then how on Earth could he beat the millions of athletes with dreams of going professional? Instead of indulging in empathy and pity for himself, he used his frustration and anger to become the best on the JV basketball team that season. Mike could have given up at this point and decided that basketball was not his forte, and that maybe he should try to succeed at something else. This would have been completely logical, would it not have? But his inner desire to succeed at basketball allowed him to transform this pain in a positive way to ensure he would never be cut again.

People are eager to change their circumstances, but uneager to change themselves first, which leaves them stagnant in their profession for years. The problem is you keep saying you want all these various external things in your life such as wealth, but you do nothing to internally change yourself first. Let's say you are working as a waiter or waitress in a restaurant, and your critical weakness is your inability to remember customers' orders. Due to your lack of service, you receive little to no tips at all, and thus you are desperate to change your circumstances. If you do nothing to change the underlying problem that you cannot remember customers' orders properly, then you will see the same problem of receiving little tips no matter what restaurant you work for. The only way to change your circumstance of receiving miniscule tips is to change yourself first – meaning, work on your inability to remember orders. Then, once you have perfected this, your circumstances will change.

Mike worked endlessly to improve his basketball game, and he trained rigorously on his own over the summer to ensure he would not hear the same words from the coach again in the fall. In order to get a different output, there needs to be a different input, and Mike understood this concept. His vigorous summer training was not required; no one told him he had to practice, he made the decision himself. It is very easy to do what your coach or parent tells you to do because you were told to do it, but the true character of a person is revealed by his actions when no one is watching over his shoulder or telling him what to do.

Mike had a desire burning within him to make the varsity team the following year, and the universe rewards action. Instead of talking about his goal of wanting to make varsity, he went out and took shot after shot to practice and train. Talking about your goals is nothing but vibrational frequencies; there is no substance without action. All the talk in the world will not change your current situation in life – the only way to change your position is to actually take action and do something about it. Stop talking the talk, and begin to walk the walk. That coming fall as a junior in high school, Mike made the varsity team.

During his junior year, Mike continued to play with a chip on his shoulder that he needed to prove his worth. He would not just go to his team's mandatory practice, but would stay after the already long practice to work on different aspects of his game that he knew needed improvement. If you are an athlete, you need to understand that every player is attending his team's mandatory practice, so how can you be better than the next player if you are doing just what the next player does? You need to put in time before or after practice to outwork your competition if you want to be better than everyone else.

After a successful junior year on the varsity squad, Mike continued to train day in and day out over the next year to position himself to have earned an opportunity to play basketball at the next level. His myriad of hours spent sweating before and after practice on the court helped him greatly improve many aspects of his basketball game, and he had a very successful senior season where he was named to the McDonald's All-American Team. Being named an All-American means that the player is one of the top in the entire country. Quite shocking how Mike's coach in his sophomore year cut him from the team because he lacked talent and was not skilled enough to play at a varsity level, and then a mere two years later he was named one of the top players in the country. Was this a surprise to Mike? Not in the slightest as Mike always knew the potential he had within him even though others could not see it, and he relentlessly committed his time to show the world what he was capable of.

Think about an area in your life where you have been told by either your friends, coaches, or family members that you do not have what it takes to be successful. Now, why would you listen to them? If Mike listened to his coach in his sophomore year and allowed those harsh words of "you are not skilled enough to play on a varsity level" control his own belief about himself, he would have never become a McDonald's All-American at this point in his life.

How did Mike do this though? How could it be that within one year he achieved these results? It is simple: he poured his heart and sweat into becoming better and better every day. Talent and skill are two completely different attributes. Talent is what you are born with, i.e. your natural abilities, but skill is developed from the relentless grind of perfecting your craft. Skill will always beat talent, so just because someone was born with more talent than you does not mean you will not outshine them some day. Talent does help, but skill is the overwhelming factor that separates an individual from being a good player or a great player. Do you think I would be writing about Mike if he stayed where he was, felt sorry for himself, and did nothing about it?

Mike continued his basketball career at one of the top universities in the country – the infamous University of North Carolina. Along with packing up his tangible belongings to bring to the university, he also brought his work ethic with him. Coming in as a freshman, Mike had a lot to prove to his coaches and new teammates. Always wanting to do more than others are willing to do, Mike focused on his basketball game like he had never done before. He earned a position as a starter on one of the top teams in the country, and he was named the ACC (Atlantic Coast Conference) Freshman of the Year.

Mike's team did extremely well that season, and they were able to work their way to the NCAA Championship game. Playing against Georgetown, another elite team, the championship game was undecidedly close. In the final seconds of the game, Mike positioned himself to take the game-deciding shot. To take the last shot in a game requires such an enormous deal of courage and self-confidence because if Mike missed, many would blame him for losing the championship game. This game-deciding shot is what would determine the outcome of their entire season... and he took it as a freshman! Can you guess the outcome by the confidence he possessed to take it? Mike made the shot and his team won the 1982 NCAA championship against Georgetown. Mike describes this shot as a changing point in his life – it changed his inner belief forever.

We all possess a belief about ourselves and our abilities, and whether it is on a conscious level or subconscious level, it exists within us. Shifting this inner belief causes a drastic shift in what we find to be acceptable and not acceptable in our life. Is it acceptable to have excessive body fat, to receive C's on your report card, and to be viewed as a liability at work by your boss? Or are you going to say that I will only accept the best in all areas of my life because I am a special individual that has chosen to achieve greatness, and I am willing to accept the sacrifices in order to achieve my dreams.

Just like Mike, we all have that turning point from one single action we take that changes our lives. All it takes is one moment to change our life's navigation. Think of it like a ship sailing on the open ocean: if we turn the sails by just one degree over the course of many miles, our navigational trail will have been completely altered over the course of many miles – caused just by one degree. This turning point gives us the confidence and belief that we are better than we believe and better than how others perceive us.

Self-confidence is like oil in a car, skills are like the gas, and your body is like the car. The car traveling is the result of you taking action to achieve your dreams, but in order to do this, you must have the proper amount of oil and gas in your car. Without the gas required to run the car, you will not be able to move. Likewise, without the skills required to achieve your dream, you will not be able to achieve them. This is where the practice comes in. You must practice over and over and over again in order to achieve mastery. With each day of practice, the car slowly fills up with gas. Even when you become an expert in your field, you need to continue practicing to maintain that level of expertise, otherwise the car will have used up all the gas and not be able to travel. However, the gas will not get your car moving alone. You need the oil as well, which represents your level of self-confidence. All the skills in the world mean nothing if you do not possess the self-confidence to showcase your abilities. Without self-confidence, there will be no action as the fear of failure or of doing the activity wrong will paralyze you. Self-confident individuals put themselves in positions to cease opportunities to make themselves successful. Even if the outcome is failure in the moment, they do not get consumed by that failure. They simply understand it is part of the process, and they continue forward. You need both self-confidence and the necessary skills to achieve your dream, like a car needs oil and gas. Then, the car moves swiftly down the road as you drive to your location, which represents your goal.

Instead of becoming complacent because he made the game-winning shot in the National Championship game, Mike continued to train as if he did not make that elusive shot to win that championship. He did not want his past successes to limit him in his future successes, so he practiced as if his team had come up short and lost. This work ethic reflected in his level of play, and he would go on to have two more stellar years of college basketball.

Instead of coming back to the University of North Carolina for his senior year, Mike decided to forgo his final year and enter the NBA draft early. Even after a remarkable collegiate career filled with numerous accolades, Mike was only drafted as the third overall pick in the NBA draft. With his reputation and skill, many speculated he would be drafted first overall; but once again, he was faced with disappointment in his life. You may be thinking that to be drafted at all is an accomplishment, but Mike held himself to a higher standard and wanted to be drafted first.

Somebody on this Earth has to be the best at a particular craft, and Mike wanted it to be him. Somebody had to be drafted as the #1 pick just like someone has to be the best coach in his sport, best salesman in his company, best teacher in his school, or any other profession on this Earth. Somebody has to be the best at it, so why can it not be you? This is the level of mindset you must possess in any profession if you want to be the best.

Many critics argued that Mike would be too skinny to excel in the NBA and that the bigger players would easily be able to push him around. If you look at pictures of Mike in the beginning of his career, he was much leaner than the other NBA veterans. So what did Mike do? He thanked his critics for pointing out a weakness of his, and he began to vigorously lift weights to ensure this would be a weakness no more.

When someone in your life points out a weakness of yours, which is going to happen countless times in your life if it has not happened already, you have two options: accept the weakness and let it control you, or turn this weakness into one of your greatest strengths. So which option will you choose?

In the NBA, Mike played every game to the best of his ability because he knew somebody somewhere was watching him play for the very first time and they would form a lasting opinion about him. This means that Mike knew there would be a fan in the stands that was watching him play for the first time, or a person watching him on TV for the first time, and that this person may or may not already have an expectation about him. If the person did have an expectation, Mike did whatever he could to ensure that he more than met that expectation, and if the person had no expectation about his level of play, he wanted to leave a miraculous impression on the person after watching the game.

It was this mindset of always giving his best regardless of how he felt physically and mentally that allowed him to have one of the most successful NBA careers in history.

This basketball player, Michael Jordan, went on to revolutionize the sport of basketball forever with millions of kids dreaming to be "Like Mike." He was a 14-time NBA all-star, six-time NBA champion, five-time NBA MVP, and two-time Olympic gold medal winner among countless other awards. Michael Jordan is considered to be one of the most well-known athletes in the history of all sports. He built a world-renown brand around himself in the apparel industry with the Nike Air Jordan shoes that are not only worn by millions, but also saved as collectible items. In 2010, Michael Jordan was ranked as the 20th most powerful celebrity in the world by *Forbes Magazine*, and in 2015, he became the first athlete in history to become a billionaire. Quite astonishing achievements in a sport where he was told he was not good enough to play, don't you think?

> *"I have missed more than 9,000 shots in my career. I have lost almost 300 games. 26 times, I've been trusted to take the game winning shot and missed. I've failed over and over and over again in my life. And that is why I succeed."*
> *– Michael Jordan*

Chapter 9

Henry – Bankrupt from His Idea

Born on a farm in Michigan, Henry came into this world in 1863. His father was an immigrant from Europe, and his mother lived a difficult life as her parents died when she was a child leaving her to eventually be adopted by her neighbors.

Henry had a very close relationship with his mother growing up, and the bond between them was inseparable. He identified himself with his mother, and she greatly supported him. On a tragic day in 1876 at 13 years old, Henry's mother died. This left him in a very saddened and depressed state of mind. Without his mother, his father expected Henry to help more with the family farm, which he would end up doing for only a short period of time as he despised farm work. Instead, he began to devote more of his time to finding what he loved to do.

If you are doing something that you do not love, you need to find exactly what it is that warms your heart whenever you talk about or engage in that endeavor. If you do not have the feeling of excitement each morning knowing that you have the opportunity to work on your current endeavor, then you are just wasting your time. You should never venture down a certain career path strictly because of the financial success it is known to bring. You are doing a disservice to yourself if you do because regardless of the current industry you are in, whether it is arts, music, athletics, academia, or any other field, you can become wealthy in it. Millions of dollars change hands in every industry each day, so money can be made in any profession. The reason why you do what you do should not be because of the money, but because it gives you meaning and purpose in your life. Once you find the endeavor that does give you meaning and you put your entire self into it, you will become successful in your industry. The money will follow when you are really good at something, it does not work in the opposite way. Money will always follow success because when you are great at what you do, you add value to society. We as humans exchange money in return for the value it adds to our life. Focus on being the best at what you do and adding real value to society, and then the money will follow.

At the age of 16 in 1879, Henry left home to work as an apprentice machinist in Detroit, and after a few years of work in this industry with two different companies, he eventually returned home in 1882 to work again on the family farm. While working on the farm, Henry began to study bookkeeping at a nearby college – taking an action necessary to change his life.

Education and knowledge are the foundations of success. You know what the greatest part about knowledge is – it is completely free. We live in a society where endless information is available at our disposable through various sources of technology. Nothing is stopping you from using your computer or cell phone to research and learn skills that will improve your abilities in your endeavors. Too many people use technology for the wrong purpose, such as useless entertainment, but the value of it lies in the plethora of knowledge it holds just waiting for us to discover. Even if you do not have a technological device, you can still access all of this information. So where is this vast amount of free information? The answer is your public library. There are plenty of public libraries containing thousands and thousands of books in a myriad of towns in every state. It does not cost any money to walk into the library, pick out a book from the shelf that interests you, and then sit down at a table and read it for the day. Instead of investing in useless entertainment, invest in your mind by reading books at your local library. An investment in your mind will be more useful than any short-term gratification that entertainment will give you.

After working on the family farm for a few more years, Henry began work as an engineer at night in 1891. Since he was working the nightshift, he would have to sleep during the day. Instead of wasting all these precious hours sleeping, Henry used this time during the day to work on a passion of his, which was gasoline engines. Through tireless effort and years of experimenting, Henry finally completed his first self-propelled vehicle that he called the Quadricycle.

While his new invention was quite an impressive feat, the environment was filled with ruthless competitors waiting to shut him down. New companies in this industry would quickly die as the competition was very cutthroat. Even though the Quadricycle looked nice and ran well, it was much too small and not efficient for large scale production. Instead of feeling sorry for himself because his first vehicle was not efficient, he used his pain as motivation to work on and design an even better vehicle. His second self-propelled vehicle was produced in 1898, and with this new invention, he was able to attract financing from one of the top politicians at the time to create the Detroit Automobile Company.

Henry did not attract the financing by saying once he got the financing then he would build the second vehicle. He put the work in of building it first in order to achieve the financing opportunity later. Most people look for the opportunity first before they want to become fully committed to their endeavor. Once again, it does not work this way in life. You will need to commit hours of sweat and pain to your craft, and only then will you create an opportunity for yourself at a later point in time.

Even with the needed financing, what happened to the Detroit Automobile Company? It ended up only producing 20 cars that were of low quality and sold at too high of a price, so two years later in 1901, the company went bankrupt.

Most people want a guarantee in knowing that there will be a definite reward at the end of all their hard work. They are afraid to take a risk because they know the possibility of failing exists, and they allow this fear to consume them. When taking risks, people crave to know that there will be a guarantee, but to bluntly tell you the truth, there are no guarantees in life. Just because you put your time and energy into something does not mean that you will be guaranteed a victory. For example, two basketball teams will practice for many hours over the course of a week to prepare for the game on Saturday, but will both teams win? Only one team will be declared victorious after the game clock expires on that Saturday. Each team has to prepare for the game with as much effort as possible, but there is no guarantee to either team that they will win. What is the other option for these teams though? They could sit around all week thinking that the practice is a waste of time because there is no guarantee they are going to win, in which case they have will have no chance of winning, or they can put in as much work as possible to prepare for that game in order to position themselves for victory.

After his company went bankrupt, Henry analyzed his failure to properly identify the mistakes he made in order to ensure that they would not be repeated in the future. After each failure you face in life, you need to objectively reflect on the failure if you ever want to achieve a different result in your next endeavor. Without proper reflection, you will keep making the same mistakes over and over again because you never identified them as being mistakes. When you were a child first learning math, if you believed 2 + 2 = 5 and every time you saw this math problem you wrote down this answer, it would be wrong every time. If your teacher never corrected you or you never identified it as being a mistake, you would accept that solution as being correct. This little problem would soon transform into a much bigger problem because larger mathematical equations could never be solved. Proper reflection means providing yourself with honest, transparent feedback. It can be painful to identify your mistakes and weaknesses, but if you do not, you will continue to bring your same mistakes to your next endeavor.

Henry started his second automobile venture in 1901, which had been reorganized from the ashes of his previous bankrupt company. After fighting with a business partner, Henry abruptly left this second company he helped create. This company would continue on without Henry, and it later changed its name to the Cadillac Motor Company.

At this point in his life, Henry had now failed twice with two different automobile companies. Despite both of these devastations, he still possessed the courage and resiliency to continue forward until he succeeded. These two tremendous failures of his provided Henry with the knowledge and experience he would not have otherwise been privileged to if he had not failed both times.

Taking another leap of faith, Henry created his third automobile venture with another business partner. Needing automotive parts to build his cars, he entered into a contract with two brothers known as the Dodge brothers who had the machines necessary to help supply his new company. With slowing sales, Henry faced yet another crisis when the Dodge brothers demanded payment for their first large shipment of supplies to the company. Since his business had not been performing, Henry had to go on a relentless quest of seeking financing in order to have the funds available to make payment. He was finally able to convince a group of investors to provide financing, and the company survived – in 1903, Henry changed the name of the company and it became permanent.

What allowed Henry to succeed with his new company was his unorthodox approach to the treatment of his employees. Promoting welfare capitalism, he took a very unusual amount of interest in the lives of all his employees and paid them a far greater amount of money than was normal at the time though he restricted their leisure hours. Giving his employees a pay that was more than double that of the other automobile companies, workers flocked to his company and Henry was able to retain the best talent. With top quality employees came lower training costs and more efficient factories since the workers were more qualified, so not only were these workers receiving far better pay, but Henry was able to run a much more efficient company. In addition, he hired women and handicapped men at a time when this was very uncommon as he always looked to help out his community.

However, Henry set personal standards for his employees that many would have found too challenging to uphold in order to have a better job (and overall better lifestyle). In order to be considered for the high pay he offered, his employees had to live a life acceptable to Henry, which meant no heavy drinking, gambling, or being a deadbeat father or mother that neglected his or her children. Henry wanted to help transform people into assets and not liabilities to society.

In 1908, Henry introduced the Model T, which was a revolutionary car in the automobile industry. This car was the first mass-produced affordable car available to many Americans, and it is the basis of the current day automobile. Not relying on just his product to promote itself, Henry ensured that every newspaper carried stories and ads about his new, innovative Model T automobile.

Being revolutionary and following his vision once again, Henry introduced moving assembly belts into his manufacturing plants in 1913, which allowed production to be much more efficient. In 1914, more than 250,000 Model T automobiles had been sold. Instead of being content with the level of success his automobile had achieved, Henry continuously worked on strategic marketing and improving the quality of his Model T automobiles, and in 1916, more than 550,000 had been sold that year – more than double the sales volume of that two years prior in 1914. As it continued to gain popularity amongst American consumers, half of all cars in America by 1918 were the Model T.

Despite this eventual success with his automobile company, the struggles would persistently continue for Henry. As the competition became fiercer and larger in size by the mid 1920's, Model T sales began to rapidly decline. This once ultra-successful automobile was losing popularity with the American public.

Once you reach success, you need to ensure that you continue to innovate and push your boundaries. If you become complacent, your competitors who are working to overtake you will surpass you, and Henry began to experiment with a new automobile that would once again revolutionize the automobile industry.

Through perseverance and an unremitting ability to work, Henry introduced the Model A in December 1927. It achieved far-greater success than the Model T, and by the time production ended in 1931, Henry had sold close to 5,000,000 Model A cars.

Even though Henry had achieved success in the automobile industry, it did not guarantee that he would achieve success in his next venture. Henry entered the aviation business and designed the first successful passenger airline, which flew 12 passengers in its first flight in June 1926. The plane, known as the Trimoter, was eventually discontinued when the company had to shut down during the Great Depression.

Just because you were successful in one endeavor does not mean success will now come easily in all your future endeavors. You need to commit just as much, if not more time and effort, to your next endeavor than your last one if you want to be victorious. Success is never easy, but that is what makes achieving it worthwhile. If it was easy to achieve success, everybody would be successful – and achievements would have no real meaning. If it was easy to be a doctor, everybody would be one. If it was easy to win a national championship, everybody would win one. If it was easy to be a billionaire, everybody would be one. Nothing great is easy, but it is worth it.

This man, known as Henry Ford, is the founder of the current day automobile. He created the Ford Motor Company, which is currently one of the largest automobile manufacturers in the world with over $138,000,000,000 in annual revenue and over 185,000 employees. He was honored by the United States Postal Service on a postage stamp from 1965 to 1978 for his revolutionary contributions to society, and in 1999, he was voted as one of the 18 profound members on the "Gallup's List of Widely Admired People of the 20th Century." Deciding to leave a legacy instead of liabilities, Henry Ford transformed what was once an expensive, luxury product into a practical form of transportation that is a staple to our everyday life.

> *"Failure is simply the opportunity to begin again,*
> *this time more intelligently."*
> *– Henry Ford*

Chapter 10

Walter – A Lack of Imagination

Born in 1901, Walter spent his early childhood years on a farm in Marceline, Missouri. He grew up in a very large family, being one of five children, and was often left to make his own decisions. As a juvenile in Missouri, Walter would develop an enthusiastic passion for drawing that would stay with him for life. His neighbor identified the artistic talent Walter enthusiastically possessed, and he would frequently pay Walter to draw pictures of his coveted pet horse.

Nothing great nor small in life was ever achieved without the key ingredient of enthusiasm. If you do not wake up in the morning with the euphoric feeling of knowing that you are following your heart and doing something that provides actual meaning to your life, then you are cheating yourself and wasting your time. Where your heart is, that is where success will lie. When you are enthusiastic about what you do, you will find any tasks related to your endeavor as being enjoyable.

While most kids begin their formal education around five years old, Walter did not begin his until eight years old in 1909. Thus, when he began his education, he was already behind his peers in general academic knowledge. Within one year, Walter would be forced to switch schools and leave his friends behind.

After his family struggled on their farm, they moved to Kansas City, Missouri in 1910. While attending school in Kansas City, Walter also worked a newspaper delivery route with very long hours. He would wake up every morning at 3:30 a.m. and deliver newspapers until the morning school bell rang, and then once school was dismissed, he would continue on his delivery route until dinner time; and Walter worked like this for over six years! At a young age, this was quite a long, exhausting day for him.

It is evident that Walter was cultivating a work ethic that would form the backbone to any endeavor he would undertake going forward. He began to develop the habit of pushing himself above and beyond what many would consider to be an uncomfortable situation, but it is this pressing and pushing that separates an individual from his peers in the most needed moment. Walter lived this lifestyle for over six years, and it became his way of life. If you do something long enough and stay committed to your commitment, your body will transform it into a habit. This can work for you or against you, so only do things that are pushing you closer towards a better life.

Despite having a dream of becoming an artist, at 16 years old in 1917, Walter dropped out of school to join the military, but was denied for being under the legal age limit. Clever as usual, he found a way around this by joining the Red Cross where he could still be involved in the war over in France as an ambulance driver. After suffering through the traumatic scenes of war in France and coming back to the United States in hopes of pursuing a career as either an ambulance driver or an artist, he had absolutely no luck in his employment search as no one wanted to hire him for either profession.

However, he was eventually hired to do temporary work as an artist for a local newspaper known as the Kansas City Star in 1919. Despite his artistic abilities, Walter was soon fired for lacking originality in his designs and for not having any good ideas. This boy whose dream was to be an artist and whose passion laid in this field was told these harsh comments. Hearing these words would crush many, especially at this age, but Walter continued forward knowing something better would lay ahead for him. Walter also applied to be a truck driver and clerk with the Kansas City Star but was turned down for both positions.

Being unemployed and desperately searching for a job, his brother was able to help him get another temporary job at an art studio creating advertisements for newspapers and movie theaters. While working at this job, Walter met a fellow cartoonist by the name of Ubbe, and they both realized the enthusiasm they shared for cartoons and drawing. Walter and Ubbe decided to take the risk of forming their own commercial cartoon company, but their initial business venture failed.

I cannot stress this point enough, failure is inevitable. There is no way to hide from it; you cannot avoid it. When you hit failure, you can either give up or keep moving forward. You need to just get up and try again until you succeed. When failure throws its knockout punch, your will and determination to succeed at your goal must be strong enough to pick yourself up and continue fighting.

After living what can be viewed as a struggling, mediocre life, his father decided to have a serious conversation with Walter about his employment prospects. He told Walter to get a very low-paying job at a factory believing the small but steady income would be much better than Walter's chase of a useless hobby. Walter replied to his father by saying he wanted to be an artist, to which his dad said "You can't make a living drawing pictures... you need a real job."

You cannot let someone else influence you and your dreams. Many people will try to persuade you that what you are attempting to achieve is impossible or not worth your time. You cannot listen to them. If you are enthusiastic about what you do and stick with it, success will come. Enthusiasm is one of the most underrated aspects in a person during any employment, athletic, or academic evaluation. Even if an individual's level of skill in a particular endeavor is not currently where it should be, if he possesses enthusiasm for whatever he is doing, it will only be a matter of time before his skill rises far above everyone else. When you are enthusiastic about something, you want to get better at it – no one needs to tell you to improve because you want to be the best and you will sacrifice whatever it takes to reach that level of mastery.

After his initial business venture with Ubbe failed, Walter created Laugh-O-Grams, which was a series of both live action and animated fairytales that were a few minutes in length. Through long, tedious hours of work, Walter was able to eventually strike a deal with a Kansas City theater to show his cartoons to the public, which was a very large step in the right direction. His animations started to become popular, and he began to experience a level of success – he soon had to hire a few employees to help out.

However, it was not long before failure would come knocking at the door once again for Walter. Overwhelmed by heavy debts, Laugh-O-Grams declared bankruptcy in 1923 and Walter was left having to start all over again.

Coming so close to success, it would have been easy for Walter to become depressed after his semi-successful company went bankrupt. It is in these moments when our mind will resort to negativity and focus on our flaws instead of our assets. The words of his father's doubt circled his mind, but he did not allow them to overpower his own beliefs.

Even though he faced failure with his now past two business ventures, Walter decided to take the risk of traveling out to Hollywood to continue to pursue his passion for cartoons. He had no money, only a few of his animations, and an inner desire to achieve success in what he was passionate about that not even bankruptcy could destroy. How many of you would take this risk again knowing that you had failed twice already in this industry?

Just because he is currently failing does not mean that he will fail forever. Your present circumstances have nothing to do with how your future will be. Just because you are failing in school, or you are a coach and your team is losing game after game, or you were just fired from your job does not mean that your life will always be miserable like this. You need to realize that if you accept your situation, you will keep it – but if you tell yourself that you deserve more and that something better is waiting for you, you will soon find it. Think of it like this, that success you want is hidden underneath something in a forest. If all you do is complain about how miserable your situation is and how difficult it is to find it in this huge forest, you will never look under anything to find the success. Without action, there can never be any positive results. Or if you are looking, you just search under the large, obvious rocks in the forest because you do not want to commit the extensive effort in trying to find the hidden success. You need to immerse yourself in action to change your circumstances by looking in areas you never thought opportunities existed, which means looking under all the little pebbles, among the piles of leaves or sticks, or even in the thorn bushes.

Out in Hollywood, Walter began to work on animation comedies known as *Alice Comedies* with his brother who also came along with him. Walter and his brother received $1,500 for their first *Alice Comedy*, which was a satisfactory start for them. Although Walter's past business ventures failed, he finally believed that these comedies would yield a different outcome and become widespread to society. However, by the time the series ended in 1927, it had completely lost popularity.

Upon the failure of his *Alice Comedies* in 1927, Universal Studios wanted to enter the cartoon business, and they sought after Walter, along with Ubbe, to draw a character for them. Walter and Ubbe tirelessly worked on creating a new, friendly cartoon, and it turned out to be Oswald the Lucky Rabbit. Their first version of the Oswald cartoon was rejected by Universal Studios as they said it was of poor quality and Oswald was sloppy. Instead of becoming angry over Universal Studios harsh words, Walter and Ubbe worked on perfecting the character into something even better, and on their tedious, second attempt of drawing it, Oswald the Lucky Rabbit became a big success and gained tremendous popularity.

Walter would now encounter one of the most difficult challenges he faced yet. With his newly designed character becoming a huge success in 1928, Walter went to negotiate a higher fee for Oswald the Lucky Rabbit. Charles, the producer of Universal Studios at the time, negated Walter's fair and righteous request for a higher fee and came back with his own unjust request. Charles proposed reducing Walter's compensation for Oswald and threatened him by saying he would open his own studio and produce the character himself if Walter did not accept. By firmly declining this new, unwarranted offer from Universal Studios, Walter lost all of his artists except for Ubbe, who stayed loyal to him regardless of the circumstances. In spite of all the time Walter spent acquiring these essential artists necessary to assist him with his animations, he would now have to begin all over again and tirelessly find new artists.

It is not what happens to us in life, but how we react to it. Walter not only lost the Oswald character he designed which gained tremendous popularity, but he lost all of his valuable artists that helped him in drawing cartoons. To make matters worse, in 1931, his wife was pregnant and suffered a miscarriage and lost their baby. Walter, being a kid at heart and always wanting children of his own, was devastated by this news. This colossal setback in his life would give him the determination and drive to create one of the most renowned cartoon characters of all time.

After losing the rights to Oswald along with his artists, Walter endlessly used his creativity to think of a new, original character that would be more popular than his previous Oswald character. After hours and hours of creative thinking, Walter came up with the idea of basing a character on the mouse he adopted as a pet while working on his Laugh-O-Grams in Kansas City. He spent significant time drawing this new character, but finally turned it into a version he was most proud of. This mouse would star in two cartoon films, *Plane Crazy* and *The Gallopin' Gaucho*, and Walter had quite the excitement that his newly designed character would become popular. To his disappointment, both films failed as no one wanted to distribute either film to the public. No distributor saw any potential in this new character of his, but Walter knew if he persisted long enough, he would make this mouse a huge success.

Walter continued to pour his time and energy into a third cartoon film featuring this new mouse character, which would be called *Steamboat Willie*, and he finally struck success. The film became a huge sensation, and in 1932, Walter received an academy award for this little mouse character, known as Mickey Mouse, that had previously failed two times.

Legacies are like a brick wall, they are built brick by brick through a continuous process of hard work and effort. Brick walls are not built over night, and neither are legacies. If you want to leave a legacy, you must work day and night to do so. Each little brick is like each moment in your life that you have the ability to utilize in order to reach your desired achievement. Having achieved a grand level of success with Mickey Mouse, Walter could have laid back, taken his foot off the pedal, and celebrated this great success; but instead, he choose to work even harder.

One of Walter's next major films was called *Flowers and Trees*. Despite the film already being more than half-way completed in black and white, Walter realized he could significantly improve the overall quality if he made it in color. So, what did he do? Walter started over from the very beginning incurring significant costs and time to make it in color.

How many of you would do this with something in your life – completely start over writing your study guide because you realized it did not have the best format, or start over on that movie you are trying to produce because you realized that the plot should be altered a little bit? If you want to achieve something great, you need to go through the sacrifices of improving it even when it seems like a massive inconvenience or waste of time. It would have been much easier for Walter to continue on with this film in black and white and not switch to color, but Walter never settled for producing something he viewed was not his best work. Anything that has your name attached to it needs to reflect your absolute best work. Your work is a direct reflection of yourself, so take pride in knowing that you did the best you could possibly do.

Flowers and Trees would go on to become an enormous success, and this was all because Walter decided to start over again and produce something of better quality. He was capable of something better, and he made sure that this capability did not just rest inside of him as his own belief of what he could produce, but was actually seen by the world.

In 1933, Walter began to work on another animated film. The production would take far longer than anticipated and the cost was far greater than it was initially budgeted. This animated film would take over three years to finish, and along the way, the cost of the production exceeded the budget by over 100%. In order to continue working on this film, Walter had to seek out loan officers for money. With only a few small cuts of the film produced, he had to convince them that his vision for the film would come to fruition and be a success. Through his determination, Walter was able to acquire the necessary loans to finish production. In 1938, this film known as *Snow White and the Seven Dwarfs* would go on to become the most successful motion picture of the year and the first cartoon film to ever win an Oscar.

Even after achieving prominent success, Walter's ideas would continue to be doubted by others. After visiting numerous amusement parks with his daughters, Walter developed an insatiable desire to build an amusement park that brought his characters to life. However, others could not see his vision and viewed it as being completely foolish. In order to build the amusement park, Walter would need a great deal of financing due to the lavish costs of construction. Each bank he went too, he would hear the same answer of "NO." Shaking off each rejection, he would eagerly move on and ask the next bank, which would give him the same exact response as the previous ones – until eventually, Walter heard that lone "yes" he so fervently waited to hear. In his extensive pursuit, Walter was rejected 302 times by banks before finally receiving the financing he needed to construct his dream park.

Think about this – even with the success he had at this point in his life, his brilliant idea was still turned down 302 times by banks. It is not the person in the fight, but the fight in the person. Walter refused to accept "NO" as an answer and kept on enthusiastically going to the next bank believing that he would eventually get the financing. All it took was a single "yes" and all 302 failures were forgotten; his endeavor of seeking the financing needed was viewed as a success.

While Walter would unfortunately pass away in 1966 before he finished building the theme park, his brother continued on with Walter's dream. Finally created in 1971, Disney World would turn into one of the most infamous amusements in the world with millions of visitors ever year. Walter lived a life filled with struggles and setbacks, but every one of these setbacks was a setup for a comeback.

During his lifetime, this man known as Walt Disney won 22 academy awards as well as seven Emmy awards for his various animated films. He built a brand that is one of the most recognizable amongst all of society as well as one of the most successful of all time. The Walt Disney Company is the best-known and most successful motion-picture company in the world, and his animated films and characters have provided happiness to billions of people. Inducted into the California Hall of Fame, Walt Disney turned numerous failed ventures into a media, merchandise, and entertainment conglomerate through decades of hard work and persistence.

> *"All our dreams can come true, if we have the*
> *courage to pursue them."*
> *– Walt Disney*

Chapter 11

Dwayne – Crushed Dreams

Born in California in 1972, Dwayne was immediately confronted with the challenges of living in an impoverished family filled with conflict. His father Rocky was a professional wrestler who traveled almost every day and had an unfaithful relationship with his wife that was eventually exposed. He very infrequently saw his son, which left Dwayne very saddened. Rocky would ultimately face serious legal charges and be blacklisted from ever wrestling again. As a result, Rocky became an alcoholic and Dwayne's relationship with his father was significantly damaged. Along with these struggles in his younger years, Dwayne was forced to move numerous times, both with his parents and without them.

After briefly living with his mother's family in New Zealand as a child and attending school there, Dwayne returned back to the United States to live with his parents. He moved yet again for his sophomore year of high school and attended school in

Hawaii. While in Hawaii, his family was evicted from their one-bedroom apartment and his mother's car was repossessed. Seeing his mother crying, Dwayne promised her he would never let this happen again in her life.

A tree is judged by the fruit it bears not the fruit that it talks about or the fruit it thinks it deserves. All the complaining and wishing in the world will never change the fact that an Apple tree produces Apples – the tree is judged by the fruit it bears. The only way to produce results in your life is to take action. While dreaming your goals or speaking them is great, you will not become any closer to them until you take that first step.

Despite his promise to his mother that times would soon get better for them, Dwayne continued to get in trouble with the law. By the time he was 17 years old, Dwayne had been arrested eight times for a variety of crimes related to theft. Due to his father's job which required their family to relocate, Dwayne moved out to Pennsylvania for his junior year of high school where he began playing football, track and field, and wrestling. He transferred his pain of living a troubled life into his sports, and he began to excel on the football field. Once he identified his passion for this sport, he began to dream of playing in the NFL, but first, he would need to prove himself at the elite collegiate level. With his athleticism and ability to push himself on the field, Dwayne received many offers to play football on the Division 1 level in college. After considering the schools, he made the decision to attend the University of Miami on a full scholarship as a defensive tackle.

Considering the University of Miami is one of the top football programs in the nation, it seemed to Dwayne that his dream of playing in the NFL could become a reality if he continued to vigorously work at his craft. After being announced as a starter in his freshman year in 1989, Dwayne was badly hurt in practice just a week before the first game of the season. Dwayne became so depressed that he cut classes and was listed on academic probation for his unbelievably low GPA of 0.7 after having failed almost all of his classes. His coach pulled him into the office telling him he would be cut from the team if he did not bring his grades up. It was at this moment where Dwayne said "I felt about as worthless as I had ever felt in my life." After getting the wakeup call he needed from his coach to turn things around in his life, Dwayne focused on improving his study habits and put a tremendous amount of effort into the classroom.

After recovering from his injury, Dwayne returned to the field and he helped his team accomplish the difficult feat of winning the national championship two years later in 1991. At this point, things looked favorable for Dwayne upon graduation as long as he continued down this course he was on; his prospects to receive a multi-million dollar contract in the NFL seemed bright.

Life punched Dwayne right in the face when he faced a back injury and four knee surgeries that kept him on the sidelines his senior year, which is the most critical year when being considered for the NFL draft. Having established a successful football career so far at the University of Miami, his senior year would be the deciding factor for making the NFL draft, but due to his injuries, he could not play. Dwayne would be replaced by another player who would turn into an eventual NFL star.

After the end of his senior season in 1995, he graduated from the University of Miami, but when it came time to receive an invite for the NFL combine, which is an important, invite-only event where players test and demonstrate their athletic ability, Dwayne did not receive an invitation. Upon the NFL draft, many of his former teammates would hear their names called, but Dwayne was never drafted.

Dwayne would be drafted to play in the CFL, which is the Canadian Football League, and unlike the NFL, it pays very little in comparison. However, players can use the CFL as a way to get noticed by NFL coaches after their collegiate career in an attempt to later play in the NFL. He was earning only $250 per week as a backup linebacker on the practice roster of a team in the CFL. Two months into the 1995 season, Dwayne was cut from the Canadian Football League, and his lifelong dream of playing in the NFL was crushed.

If you ever reached a point in your life like Dwayne, where a dream you had was utterly crushed, you have two options – you can either let it break you or you can allow it to be your break-through. Many people chose the easy option of letting it break them, and as a result, squander their time by sleeping and doing nothing all day. Will sleeping all day do anything to improve your current reality? The more you sit around depressed and fail to take any meaningful action, the later it will be before your current state of being changes. You must have the tenacity to get up when it feels like your world is crashing down, punch life back in the face, and demand success out of it.

Without football in his life, Dwayne felt a loss of identity. For over 10 years, Dwayne endured grueling practices day in and day out. To Dwayne, it seemed like all his hard work got him nowhere and that he was a failure. He had only one shot of attaining his dream of playing in the NFL, and he completely failed by getting quickly cut from a practice roster in the CFL, which is far less challenging than the NFL.

Having failed at what appeared to be his only way out to a better life, Dwayne moved back in with his parents in 1996 at 24 years old with only $7 in his pocket – he was completely broke. Despite the fact he had no money, he told himself "I'm broke as hell, and one day I won't be."

Living in his parents' house with no money to his name, Dwayne began to face his own serious disappointment. He already had numerous arrests at that point in his life including theft and assault, and he felt like a total failure. Dwayne began to battle depression, and he felt so disappointed that he would often spend many days crying. He saw himself for where he currently was – no job, crushed dreams, and a mental state of mind that was deteriorating.

Anybody can do well when things are going well, but it is the true character of a person that is shown when things are crashing down in his life. When things are going well, a happy state of being comes naturally and doing well for the most part is easy. It is the times when everything seems to be going against you where your true character will be put to the test. After slowly taking five steps up that mountain, you tripped and stumbled and fell down 10 steps. Do you have the resiliency to brush yourself off and continue climbing, or are you going to allow this one stumble, even though it was double in size relative to your ascent, thwart you in your conquest to the top of the mountain?

Dwayne finally made the decision to start over, rebuild himself, and remove all feelings of self-pity about his situation. He asked his father Rocky to teach him all he knew about wrestling (his grandfather also wrestled as well). His father initially resisted, but Dwayne persistently kept asking him, and finally one day, he agreed to teach Dwayne – but he told Dwayne he would not go easy on him.

Learning some of the skills from his father, Dwayne tried to find any place to showcase his new talents. With no one interested, Dwayne eventually resorted to wrestling at flea markets for only $40 a night.

Dwayne knew success is a process – there is no shortcut, and if you try to find one, you will only lead yourself down a path that will shortcut your accomplishments. You need to pay the price in order to achieve success in this give and take world. You give your time, energy, and effort to something and in return, you will eventually receive success.

After wrestling at flea markets for a very low wage, Dwayne was finally able to land a few tryouts for the WWF (World Wrestling Federation, now known as the WWE). Wrestling under the name "Flex Kavana," Dwayne was eventually able to sign a contract with the WWF. With a changed ring name, Dwayne made his WWF debut in 1996 as "Rocky Maivia," which was a combination of the ring names used by his father and grandfather. Fans of the WWF rejected him for they believed he had a cheesy character, and it was common to hear the chant "Die, Rocky, die!" or "Rocky sucks!" from the audience during his matches.

In the pursuit of your dreams, you will come across a lot of people that hate you or try to take you down. It is inevitable, no matter how hard you try, to be liked by every single person you run into in your life. Most of the time, these people hate you because you are accomplishing something they wish they could accomplish. Instead of lashing out at these haters, understand what they are there for, which is to point out your weaknesses and try to stop you from becoming successful. There is a reason why your haters have heard of you but you have not heard of them.

Dwayne lost the Intercontinental Championship of wrestling in 1997 and also suffered a knee injury in a match later that year. Upon his return, he came back in a new role as a "heel" – a heel is considered to be the antagonist in wrestling. As a heel, Dwayne refused to go by his previous ring name of "Rocky Maivia," and instead chose to cleverly narrate himself in the third person under a new ring name which would remain with him.

As his popularity with fans grew in 1998, Dwayne called himself "The People's Champion" and as a result, he would often have feuds with the owner of the WWF who said Dwayne had problems with people. Instead of accepting the owner's belief, he chose to think of himself differently and embraced a feeling that the audience loved him, which came to be.

After a highly successful wrestling career, Dwayne used his momentum to land minor roles in music videos and even hosted Saturday Night Live in 2000. Putting as much time into acting as he did to succeed in wrestling, Dwayne finally made his movie debut in *The Mummy Returns* in 2004. From the time he began his acting career in 2000, it took him over four years of working on his acting abilities to finally make a brief appearance in a movie. He seized the opportunity thanks to all of his preparation before that moment, and he was able to run with this opportunity.

Dwayne Johnson, otherwise known as "The Rock" from his time in the WWE, is widely considered to be one of the best professional wrestlers in history having 17 championship reigns in the WWE. In the year 2000, Dwayne "The Rock" Johnson co-wrote an autobiography that became #1 on the New York Time's Best Seller List for several weeks. He is currently one of the highest paid actors in Hollywood, and he has been nominated for countless acting awards over the years. He has appeared in a number of successful hits such as *The Scorpion King*, *Gridiron Gang*, *The Game Plan*, *Hercules*, and the *Fast & Furious* series. Looking to give back to society, he founded the Dwayne Johnson Rock Foundation, which is a charity aimed at helping at-risk and terminally ill children. In 2014, he became the host of the new T.V. reality series "Wake Up Call" to help transform the lives of troubled youth and put an end to their bad behavior. With so much life still ahead of him, Dwayne "The Rock" Johnson is still in the process of creating his legacy.

"I grew up where, when a door closed, a window didn't open. The only thing I had was cracks. I'd do everything to get through those cracks – scratch, claw, bite, push, bleed. Now the opportunity is here. The door is wide open and it's as big as a garage."
– Dwayne "The Rock" Johnson

Chapter 12

Joanne – A Rejected, Single Mother

J oanne was born in England in 1965. During her childhood years, she moved towns and changed schools twice. Moving as a young child can be very difficult because once established friends become lost, and it can be hard for a child to establish their social comfort zone all over again.

Feeling a bit disconnected to her classmates because she was always the shy, quiet kid, Joanne developed a passion for books and realized at a young age that she wanted to become a writer. As a child, she would always write short stories and had a very creative imagination.

Having a creative imagination is critical if you want to be an innovator or maverick in society because you will have the ability to envision yourself in a different state of being other than what you are currently living. Before you go to bed at night, spend five minutes using your imagination to envision what your life will look like when you have achieved that goal of yours. Think about all the little details behind achieving it. For example, if your goal is to graduate college, do not just envision the diploma in your hand at graduation, but visualize all your peers around you as you shake the hand of the university president, all the parents in the crowd applauding as you walk by, all the photos you will take afterwards, and all the other small details about your surroundings that will go along with receiving that diploma.

Joanne's teenage years were very unhappy. She was teased in school for her last name, and at home, her life became very complicated when her mother became ill – and the disease only worsened, which placed a tremendous amount of strain on Joanne's relationship with her father. It would have been very easy for Joanne to lash out at others for the pain she was going through, but that would have done absolutely nothing to change her situation. It would only result in her being in a worse situation for she would have alienated those outside of her family who were close to her by transferring her internal frustrations onto them. If you take your anger out from work on your family or vice versa, you will soon create two areas of your life where you will feel pain.

In 1982, Joanne took the entrance exam to try to gain admittance to Oxford University, one of the top universities in Europe, but unfortunately she was not accepted. Joanne could look at this denial in two ways – either she missed out on the opportunity to attend Oxford University or Oxford University missed out on the opportunity of having her as a student. The event itself does not define this answer, but it is Joanne who makes the decision on what she will believe.

Joanne decided to attend the University of Exeter, located in the United Kingdom, and graduated in 1986. Upon graduation, Joanne moved to London where she accepted a position of employment at Amnesty International working as a researcher and bilingual secretary – not the highest of positions by any measure. Her then current boyfriend soon moved to Manchester, thus forcing Joanne to take a lengthy train ride from London to see him on the weekends.

On one particular weekend in 1990, Joanne had a revelation that altered the course of her life. After arriving at the local train station to take a trip from Manchester back to London, she found out her train was severely delayed. With what ended up being an over four-hour delay, an idea struck Joanne while patiently waiting for the train that she should write a novel. Not only did the overall idea of the novel strike her, but it came in total form in her mind exactly how she wanted the plot to be arranged. When she finally reached her destination in London, Joanne immediately wrote down all her thoughts and soon began writing the novel. Without any money to afford a computer, she would have to write on an old manual typewriter.

We all have moments in life where we unexpectedly conjure up an idea to do something – whether it is a new invention, new technique to pitch your product, or something else. When you are given this revolutionary idea, what will you do with it? Most people will just think about it in that moment, possibly even believing it is a worthwhile venture to pursue, but quickly fears and negative thoughts creep in and negate their ability to act on it, and so the idea quickly fades from their mind. When you feel these fears of taking action, feel them and then do it anyway. You need to come to the realization that fears are made up in the mind – they are simply a figment of the imagination. Thus, our fears pertain to something in the future that has not and may not ever happen.

This new idea consumed Joanne's mind, and she was soon fired for excessive daydreaming while working at Amnesty International. She then decided to move in with her boyfriend in Manchester where she began work at the Manchester Chamber of Commerce. Similar to her last job, Joanne would also be fired from this new employment position. To make matters worse, Joanne's mother died later this year after suffering from a long, chronic illness. Being close to her mother, this left Joanne dev-astated, and it greatly affected her writing which she was already a few months into. Her mother's death left such an impact on her that she stopped working on her book and sank into a deep depression.

As humans, we have the ability to control our reaction to an event. A death is something that is very tragic and the grieving can often last a long time, but when something happens in your life that you perceive to be negative and out of your control (because we perceive whether any event is good or bad), you can always control how you will react to the event. Let's say your business goes bankrupt – you can either let this bankruptcy control your life or you can control your reaction to the bankruptcy. When you make the decision to control your reaction, you will begin to control what happens in your life around you.

Joanne would soon move to Portugal where she would teach English as a foreign language believing that the act of teaching would help her overcome her depression. Teaching her classes at night, she would work on her novel during the day making the decision to sacrifice her sleep and leisure time. The pain of these sacrifices did not compare to the drive within her to follow her dream of finishing her novel.

At the age of 27 in 1992, Joanne married a television journalist and she had her first daughter a year later in 1993. Shortly after the birth of her beautiful daughter, Joanne and her husband separated and she was left to raise the child on her own as a single mother. With no money to support her child and a novel which after three years of work was still nowhere close to being finished, Joanne and her newborn daughter moved in with her sister in Scotland.

Joanne now reached a point in her life where she viewed her-self as being a complete failure. Having graduated from the University of Exeter seven years prior, Joanne came to the realization that she was living a nightmare of a life. Her marriage had failed, she was a single mother who was jobless and did not have the ability to support her child, and she had an idea for a novel that had failed to make any significant progress. In order to provide for herself and her daughter, Joanne was forced to sign up for welfare benefits.

During this yet another dark period for Joanne, she was diagnosed with clinical depression and even contemplated suicide. Self-inflicted pain is never the solution to any problem; it only makes two problems out of what started as one problem. It is the coward's way out of dealing with pain, and these types of thoughts should never even cross your mind regardless of the challenges or disappointments you face.

Despite experiencing failure in all aspects of her life, Joanne described her failures as liberating because they allowed her to focus more on her writing. Instead of focusing on all that was going wrong in her life, Joanne began to see it as an opportunity to improve.

When you argue for your limitations, you get to keep them. If you keep telling yourself that you are overweight, lack intelligence, or are broke, you will keep these limitations with you. What you say about yourself is what you will become. Instead of always saying negative affirmations, begin to repeat positive affirmations about yourself and you will soon embody this belief, and as a result, you will eventually possess these positive attributes.

To make Joanne's situation even worse, her estranged husband had followed her and her daughter to Scotland causing Joanne nothing but more stress and problems. Joanne filed a restraining order against him and they officially divorced in 1994.

Once again, despite the upsetting circumstances surrounding her life, Joanne continued to work relentlessly on her novel. Her days would be consumed with writing, and she would sacrifice her leisure hours choosing to instead work. Five years after she first began working on it, Joanne had finally finished her book in 1995 on an old manual typewriter.

When you decide to take action towards your dream, do not immediately focus on achieving the overall grand picture of it, but rather break up your goal into many small tasks. It is much easier to focus on accomplishing each small task than it is the entire goal. With each completed task, it will give you the confidence to continue working at the next task and the next task – until one day, you have finally achieved that large goal. Achieving your goal, whatever it may be, is the result of many little successes overtime. When a farmer wants to have a great harvest of crops in the fall, he has to begin planting his seeds in the spring. Each little activity over the coming months is what will determine whether his large goal of having a successful harvest is achieved. He needs to prepare the land for planting, plant each seed into the ground, water and care for the seeds, and then pick each crop in the fall. The farmer has to pay the price all year of dedicating his time and effort to his crop by doing all the little things right, and then in the fall he reaps the large reward of a successful harvest.

After finally finishing her book with great excitement, Joanne reached out to an agent whom she would need to represent her in order to present her manuscript to a publishing house to have it published into a book. Having committed five long years of hard work into this novel, all twelve publishing houses that received her manuscript rejected her. Refusing to listen to the opinions of these publishing houses that review thousands of manuscripts each year, she decided to listen to her own belief that her manuscript would be a success.

She continued to have her agent contact publishers, and after two years of rejections, she was able to finally get one publisher to say "yes" in 1997 at 35 years old. How many of you would have persisted through two years of rejection? Joanne suffered the pain of rejection each day in order to never suffer the regret of tomorrow thinking "what if?" The "what if" question we ask ourselves after we choose not to act on something we feel we should have acted on will haunt and nag at us for life. It is always better to know the answer regardless of what it may be then to live with the possibility of regret in not taking action.

While Joanne did finally hear the "yes" she was looking for, the publisher paid her only $4,000 upfront for her novel. He also told her to get a day job because she had little, if any, chance of making money in children's books. The only publisher that was willing to publish her novel did not even believe in her, and she also had to change her pen name (meaning the name of the author published on the book) for fear that boys would not read a fiction book written by a woman.

Five months after having her novel published in 1997, it received its first award, and there would be no turning back. Shortly after, the rights to her novel were purchased in the United States in 1998 for $105,000. Joanne's novel soon became an enormous hit in the U.S.

Continuing off the success of her first book, Joanne, otherwise known as J.K. Rowling, would dedicate her life over the coming years to write seven more books in what is known as the *Harry Potter* series.

Joanne "J.K." Rowling would become the first person to ever become a billionaire by writing books. She sold over 400,000,000 copies of *Harry Potter*, and it has become the best-selling book series in history. Her final book in the series, *Harry Potter and the Deathly Hollows*, broke the sales record as the fastest selling book of all-time having sold 11,000,000 copies the first day in the United States and United Kingdom. *Harry Potter* would become a film series sensation and turned into the highest grossing film series of all-time. In October 2010, Joanne "J.K." Rowling was named the "Most Influential Woman in Britain." Known for her philanthropy as well, she has donated millions of dollars to various charities in an effort to improve our society. From being a single mother with no job or money, Joanne "J.K." Rowling defeated her challenging circumstances and failures and achieved grand success.

> *"It is impossible to live without failing at something,*
> *unless you live so cautiously that you might as well*
> *not have lived at all, in which case*
> *you have failed by default."*
> *– Joanne "J.K" Rowling*

Chapter 13

Milton – Repetitive Failures

Born in 1857, Milton was raised in rural Pennsylvania as the only surviving child of his parents. Milton's father was always looking for a "get rich quick scheme," and thus his father switched professions numerous times. As a result, their family moved frequently, which directly affected Milton's education as he was constantly switching schools. It also put great strain on his parents' weak marriage, which ultimately led to Milton's father leaving his family, forcing Milton's mother to raise him alone.

By the time Milton was 13 years old, he had already attended six different schools and had very little formal education. After many struggles in the classroom, Milton dropped out after finishing the fourth grade in 1871 (he was 14 years old vs. the normal age of around 10 years old for a fourth grade student). His mother, who was solely raising him at this point, thought it was best for him to focus on a trade and become the best at it; so she began to instill the values of hard work in him. His mother understood that if Milton possessed the work ethic needed to succeed, he would be able to achieve success once he finds his life's passion.

Regardless of your profession, the only way to achieve success is through cultivating and instilling the proper values. An individual must diligently perform his task in an efficient manner, labor lengthy hours, and work to resolve any issues that may arise while on the job – these attributes apply to a career as a postman, electrician, or investment banker. If an individual possesses the needed attributes required to be successful, he can triumph in any profession – it will only depend on where his passion lies.

Milton initially took a job in the printing industry where he would help load paper and ink into a printer, but he found this work to be very monotonous. Realizing this work did not provide any meaning to his life, he quickly switched jobs and tried working for a candy shop in an area of Pennsylvania known as Lancaster. He learned the art of candy making, creating numerous sweets such as caramels and peppermints. It was at this job that he was struck with the sensation that he loved making candy and that he had found what he wanted to do for the rest of his life.

In your life, it may take many attempts in order to find what your life's passion is, but once you do, your life will proceed on a new navigational course. It can often takes years to figure out what the endeavor is that you are passionate about, so you do not need to feel obligated to find it by a certain age. The process cannot be rushed, but rather discovered only through having the courage to try new things and put yourself into uncomfortable situations. Of course Milton felt nervous at his first day or even first week at the job in this candy shop. He was not born with the knowledge of knowing how to make candy, so it would be apparent that he would need to be taught. Do not be afraid of trying something new simply because you do not have any skill in that area, that should be a given. The only way to ever become great in any endeavor is to get started – because if you do not get started, you will never have the chance to become great.

Instilled with his mother's values of hard work, Milton spent four years working in this candy shop in order to understand the exact process of how candy is made. But Milton had a drive to make it on his own; so in 1876, he took the risk of starting his own candy shop. Without any money to his name, Milton had to borrow $150 from his aunt and uncle to turn his idea into a reality. He would have much more to learn before he was ready to run a successful candy shop as this venture failed shortly after it started.

Milton then went out to Colorado where he reunited with his father and he took another job at a candy shop. It was at this job that he learned how to make caramel and that fresh milk makes the best tasting candy; however, he would not apply this new knowledge to his candy making for a few years. He soon moved to Chicago to start up another candy shop, but shortly after opening, it failed. He quickly bounced back from this failure and decided to take the risk of opening another candy shop, this time in New Orleans, but it also failed. With two tremendous defeats in two very large cities, would Milton allow himself to get depressed and feel sorry for all of his devastating failures? Absolutely not – he continued trying until his efforts were successful.

With an excitement that he could finally succeed if he was situated in the largest candy market in the world, he traveled to New York City and opened yet another candy shop. He positioned himself in an area where failure could be said to be impossible because he was in the largest candy market in the world. Relentlessly working at his shop over 16 hours a day, Milton saw little success and his candy shop soon failed.

Positioned in the best possible market, how is it that Milton could have failed yet again? As you can see, it is not the resources around you, but how resourceful you are with those resources. Milton entered a market that had large demand on the positive side, but on the negative side, it had many competitors since it was the best area to set up shop. In order to capitalize in this candy market, he would need to find a competitive advantage over the other shops that would make his candy proprietary.

In the pursuit of your dream, you will battle against many others who possess the same goal as you. What will you do to ensure you have a competitive advantage over them? The only way it will happen is if you do things others will not do in order to achieve results others will not have. This may mean spending hours redesigning your already successful product, taking out books at the library to thoroughly read more about that law case for your studies, or seeking new ways to better teach the academic curriculum to your students.

It is now 1886 and Milton is almost 29 years old. All he has achieved in his life so far is failure, and his relatives only see him based on his past performances, not on his future potential that would soon be discovered. His father viewed him as irresponsible, and Milton was shunned by his uncles for his failed ventures that they had invested in. However, Milton chose to ignore these opinions and continue to carve out his own legacy.

What you need to realize is that someone's opinion of you does not have to become your reality. Just because someone puts limiting beliefs on you does not mean you should accept those beliefs. It is your decision whether you will listen to what others say about you or whether you will make the decision to listen to your own inner self about who you are and what you are capable of.

Upon his failure in New York City, Milton returned home to Lancaster, Pennsylvania where he had worked some years ago. Once again, Milton took the risk of starting his own company and founded the Lancaster Caramel Company. Using his knowledge from working in the Colorado candy shop that fresh milk makes the best tasting candy, he implemented this strategy into creating caramel and soon began to profoundly sell it. As soon as he had enough money from this newly started company, he paid off his debtors from his previously failed New York City candy business even though he had no obligation to do so.

In 1894, Milton began to add chocolate to the caramel he was selling and a new company began to emerge that solely focused on designing chocolate to be used with the caramel at his Lancaster Caramel Company. He worked tirelessly on both companies, and in 1900, he sold his caramel company for $1,000,000.

Persistence is vital if you want to be great at whatever your passion is. You could possess all the skill in the world, but if you are not persistent and do not keep working at it, many other individuals who possess far less abilities will outshine you simply because they stuck with it when you did not. Each day is an opportunity to improve, so each day you do not work on your dream is one more day until you will eventually reap the benefits. Your goal, regardless of how grand the endeavor is, can be achieved if you are persistent.

The Lancaster Caramel Company was built from the ashes of his previous candy shops that had failed and his crushed dreams. The failure pushed him to think in ways he had never thought before, which allowed him to achieve results he had never achieved before. Insanity is defined as doing the same thing over and over again and expecting different results. Milton had failed twice already in this industry, so instead of resorting to his previous methods of just selling candy, he looked to implement a new strategy in designing caramel.

Upon the sale of his caramel company, Milton was able to acquire a large portion of farm land out in Pennsylvania that would provide him with an adequate amount of milk to allow him to perfect the milk chocolate he had begun making in 1894.

At this time, chocolate was viewed as a luxury product sold only by the Swiss, so most average consumers did not consume chocolate like they do today. Through a relentless process of trial and error, Milton finally perfected a delicious milk chocolate formula that was affordable to the masses. But it was his failures in this trial and error process and his resilience to not give up that allowed this successful milk chocolate formula to emerge.

In 1900, Milton produced the first Hershey's chocolate bar, but his innovation did not stop there. He later went on to create Hershey's kisses in 1907, and a Hershey bar with almonds in 1908. This man, known as Milton Hershey, had pioneered an entirely new industry with his new business, the Hershey Company, which was enrooted with the belief that quality products and the well-being of employees are far more important than profits.

Even though Milton Hershey was scarcely educated and dropped out after the fourth grade, he knew the importance of education, and he wanted to make it a priority to others. He would spend a large amount of his fortune on building a successful school to help educate orphan boys and girls known as the Milton Hershey School. Since Milton was never able to have children with his wife, he wanted to ensure he gave back by helping out the children in his community.

Milton Hershey was a compassionate humanitarian, and upon the death of his wife in 1915, he transferred the majority of his assets to his Milton Hershey School trust fund. He built the town of Hershey, Pennsylvania with his resources by building houses, a post office, churches, and schools. Remarkably, during the Great Depression in the 1930's, Milton Hershey wanted to help his community that was greatly struggling so he ignited a mini-boom in his town's economy by having men construct a community building, a large hotel, and new offices for the Hershey Company in order to keep unemployment low.

Through his unrelenting drive to achieve success in the candy business and his resiliency to follow his passion despite his failures, Milton Hershey revolutionized the chocolate industry with the Hershey Company, which is currently the largest producer of chocolate in North America and a global leader in the industry.

"My success is the result of not being satisfied with mediocrity, and in making the most of my opportunities."
– Milton Hershey

Chapter 14

Eric – A Homeless, High School Dropout

Raised in the suburbs of Detroit, Michigan, Eric grew up in very unfortunate circumstances. He was raised by a teenage mom, who was 17 years old at the time of his birth, and his eventual stepfather who would come into his life later during his childhood.

In his teenage years, Eric began to hear rumors that his father was not actually his maternal father like he had always thought. One day, he angrily came home from school and asked his parents for the truth. To his shocking discovery, Eric was told his father was actually his stepfather.

Upon hearing the news, Eric could not get over the fact that his maternal father did not care enough to be in his life; he felt a sense of betrayal and abandonment. Along with the pain of feeling abandoned by his maternal father, Eric could not understand how his mother could hide this from him all his life. Negative emotions consumed his mind and body; Eric felt as though he would never be able to accept his new reality. As a result, he began to fight with his mother and stepfather, and he started failing classes at school. At this point in his life, Eric would be viewed by many as an "at risk teenager."

At 16 years old, the pain he was suffering caused him to flunk school and rebel against authority, so Eric made the decision to drop out of high school and run away from home. With absolutely no resources, Eric had to resort to living in abandoned buildings in the Detroit suburbs. The only way for him to stay alive was to eat out of garbage cans, so this became his main source of food. All the while, he was looking to escape his reality instead of accepting it for what it was. Eric cannot change the past – the only thing he can control at this point is his future.

Detroit is known for its brutally cold winters, and Eric describes this year of living on the streets in the harsh winter as one of the toughest in his life. With several feet of snow on the roads and the abandoned buildings he slept in being just as cold as the outside temperature, Eric spent many sleepless nights shivering from the fierce cold and the roaring hunger in his stomach.

After living on the streets for a year, he met a pastor who would change his life. This pastor realized the great potential within Eric, but he needed Eric to realize it himself in order to unlock that greatness. The pastor was able to convince Eric to work towards a high school education, and through immense hard work, Eric was able to complete his GED. At this point in time, he was the first man in his family in two generations to graduate from high school. Eric's maternal father had not graduated from high school, and neither had his grandfather. Eric was entering into uncharted territory and was forging a path for his own kids to follow one day. Uncharted territory is a place where fears and doubts blossom. Eric felt these emotions when he was studying for his GED, but he persisted anyway.

It would have been so easy for Eric to follow his father and grandfather's footsteps and be a permanent high school dropout – and for a very long time, he was following that path. But that would have been the easy decision, and it sounded like a worthwhile excuse to him up until he went back to get his GED. But Eric did not want to succumb to being labeled both a quitter and dropout, so he made the decision to make something of his life.

Eric understood the life motto of "if it was easy, then everybody would do it." Society prefers to engage in tasks that are easy and avoid those which are difficult. There is a reason why the bottom is overcrowded in life, because the only way to get to the top is by traveling the lonely road of hard work. If it was easy to become a millionaire, everyone would be one. If it was easy to be a straight A student, everyone would be one. If it was easy to have the body of a fitness model, everyone would have one. Too many times people turn back and give up when things become so difficult it seems like nothing can go right, but that is the defining moment when you must not quit. Pain is temporary, but if you quit and give up, that feeling will last forever.

After receiving his GED, Eric attempted to obtain his college degree, and this would be the most difficult feat of his life. He would flip flop between being committed and not committed to this degree, but it was not until the point where he immersed himself in his studies that he rapidly worked towards his degree. To obtain a four year college degree, it took Eric 12 years – 12 years to obtain a four year degree! Think about that.

How many of you would have made the decision to quit after the fifth, or sixth, or seventh year? But this is why, regardless of the situation and how bad it currently is, you must never quit. Even though he kept struggling to obtain that degree, he was finally able to do it, and this perseverance he cultivated allowed him to forge a path to success that he could apply to other areas of his life going forward.

While in the 12-year process of obtaining his undergraduate degree, he began to do public speaking as he really enjoyed speaking to others. He spoke at elementary schools, middle school clubs, or any other place that would be willing to hear his voice and his encouraging messages.

Once again, we are all given opportunities, no matter how small, but too many times we fail to see them as opportunities. Eric could have turned them down wanting to just get the big opportunity, but it was the little opportunities at these elementary schools that prepared him and built the character within him that would be needed for the big opportunities later on. It took Eric 20 years of working on his dream of being a motivational speaker before eventually becoming very popular in 2010 on YouTube. While his new motivational uploads now receive many views, when he first joined YouTube in 2008, his videos barely received any views at all.

Stop waiting to become successful overnight – it will never happen like that. It may seem like individuals in life just blew up and achieved success instantly, but it was years of practice in their private time that the world never saw that allowed them to be in an eventual position to be rewarded publicly. Success happens as a result of continuously working at your dream and doing all the little things right, and then one day, the little things add up to something monumental.

This man is Eric Thomas, otherwise known as "E.T." or "E.T. the Hip Hop Preacher." Eric has now positioned himself as one of the top motivational speakers in the world with a following of over 300,000 on YouTube. And as a result of his successes, he has become a millionaire in the process – but he still continues to start his day at 3:00 a.m. with a hunger to achieve even more. He has also created his own clothing line, his own line of motivational music, and he just recently earned a PhD. Eric Thomas has spoken to the top collegiate and professional athletic programs in the country, Fortune 500 companies, and some of the most successful individuals in the world. This is the same man who failed over and over again at a young age and dropped out in high school to live homeless on the streets of Detroit. Just because you have failed in your life does not mean you are a failure. It is not a matter of how we start, what matters is how we finish.

"It's realizing that a great dream is not as good as a great memory. The dream can be had by anyone. The memory – must be made."
– Eric Thomas

Chapter 15

Jim – Extreme Poverty

J im was born in Canada in 1962 to his parents Percy and James. Growing up, his father had a regular job as an accountant in order to support Jim and his three other siblings.

Jim realized at a young age that he was an extrovert who had an ability to make others laugh around him. At 10 years old, Jim mailed his resume to the Carol Burnett Show, which was a famous comedic television show at the time. Even though he never heard back, Jim always possessed the important attribute of hope.

Hope is something that negative people cannot take from you regardless of what they say or do. As long as you believe something better awaits you, nothing that happens can affect your hope in knowing that your treasures of the future are waiting. Hope is far more powerful than fear, and thus it is those who possess hope that will not only survive but thrive past the difficulties they are currently facing. All major successes began with the simple ingredient of hope. So as you progress on your journey towards achieving your goals, you must always have that internal hope that your dreams will soon become reality.

In junior high school, Jim was given permission to perform a standup comedy routine in front of his classmates in exchange for his good behavior in the classroom. He realized his passion lied in the comedy profession and that he could use humor to free people from their daily concerns. This identification of his passion gave Jim's life purpose unlike his father who had unfortunately given up on his own dreams. Jim's father had always dreamed of becoming a musician, but he sacrificed these dreams in order to have a "steady" job as an accountant so that his family could live with enough financial security. Up until this point, Jim's father was able to provide his family with a lower middle-class lifestyle, but soon they would face severe financial difficulties.

In 1974 at the age of 12, Jim's father lost his "steady" job as an accountant. Seeing his father lose his job while having given up on his dream in the process created a motivation within Jim that would remain with him for the rest of his life. Jim always wanted to ensure that he chased after his dream unlike his father who had chosen a different path and still ended up facing failure in something he did not enjoy doing.

With his father now unemployed, Jim's family faced overwhelming complexities. Their financial situation critically worsened and they had to do whatever it took to survive. After moving to a poor suburb in Toronto, Jim was forced to take a job as a janitor in order to help support his family. He would work an eighthour shift after school ended, and as a result his grades began to suffer. After not being able to deal with the pressures of his eighthour cleaning shift and school, Jim dropped out of high school in 1977 at 15 years old. He continued with his job as a janitor, and he often had a baseball bat on his cart because he was so angry at the world that he just wanted to beat something. At the same time, to make the situation even worse, his mother was battling a chronic illness. It was at this point that Jim and his family had to live out of a van in order to survive.

During this period, Jim became very pessimistic and angry as reflected by the baseball bat he carried around with him. He viewed the world in a very negative way – instead of having a view that the world was working towards him, he saw it as the world was working against him. How he perceived his current reality shaped his actions, which was the driving factor behind him dropping out of school. Good thoughts will never produce bad actions, and bad thoughts will never produce good actions – what you think is what will come to be. If you perceive the circumstances around you as being negative, you will become negative and attract negative things into your life. It does not matter how gloomy and depressing your situation is, you must always strive to produce good thoughts in order to achieve good actions as a result.

After dropping out of high school in 1977, he began to work on his personality impressions with his father. Jim knew he possessed talent and passion as a comedian, but he needed an opportunity to showcase his talents. After dedicating endless time to his comedic standup work, he finally got his first gig later that year at 15 years old at a comedy club in Toronto. This was his first moment to experience success in his desired field, and he wore a yellow suit his mother had sewn him.

After rehearsing his skit numerous times and entering the club with excitement, can you guess his outcome? Jim completely flopped, and his performance was considered to be awful. Having bombed his first debut as a comedian, it gave Jim serious doubt whether he would be able to make a living as an entertainer someday.

It would have been so easy for Jim to try something else at this point, but something kept nagging at him internally to continue despite his awful first performance. When you take the risk of any endeavor, there are two types of pain you can go through – either the pain of progress or the pain of failure. Jim chose the pain of progress, and even though the only signs shown to him so far were of utter failure, he knew that each passing day was a chance to improve. If Jim gave up at this point, he would never be remembered. Did you hear about the guy that gave up? No you did not? Cause no one else did either.

In 1979, Jim collected up enough courage to take the risk of moving out to Los Angeles in order to position himself to become an entertainer. After doing standup comedy at a local club and finally seeing some small success, Rodney Dangerfield (a legendary comedian) noticed him and was impressed by his acts. Rodney signed him for his opening act, which is the act prior to the main comedian's performance, for a one year period.

All Jim needed was one lucky break, but he was the one to make that lucky break. There is no such thing as luck in the world because every action is preceded by an action. Your previous actions allowed you to be in a position to get that "lucky break" needed, but had you not stayed committed and prepared yourself for that moment, this opportunity others identify as your lucky break would have never presented itself. People will say you are lucky when you have achieved something, but that is because they did not see all the practice beforehand to position yourself to be ready for that opportunity. If you are a football coach and one of your defensive backs intercepts a pass at the end of the game to win, that is not a lucky break for the coach. The coach had properly prepared his player both physically and mentally in practice for that moment to intercept the pass at the end of the game. His player knew exactly where to be because of all the practice he put in before that moment. The coach and player had properly prepared, and when the opportunity came to the player, he was ready for it because of all the preparation before that interception.

After his standup comedy gig with Rodney Dangerfield, Jim was able to appear in a few movies over the next couple years, but all of them turned out to be unsuccessful. Instead of viewing his roles in these unsuccessful opportunities as a waste of time, Jim took the view that they provided him with the necessary experiences to succeed at a later point in life.

Your recent failure in your endeavor provided you with the experiences you needed for a greater opportunity down the road. There are no shortcuts to success – nothing will be given to you, you have to earn everything. The only place success comes before work is in the dictionary, so if you want to achieve something, you need to put in the work first. You keep saying if you become that lawyer, professional coach, or doctor you will then put in the work, but it does not work that way. You need to give first in order to receive – that is how the world works. If you want to become a lawyer, you must put in the work of studying day and night in order to pass your bar exam. You cannot say let me just be a lawyer first then I will put the time in studying cases – you must put in the work of studying first and then you will become a lawyer. Once you get this concept of work first then success, you will begin to notice change in your life.

In 1984, Jim had what finally appeared to be a great opportunity. He had a big screen debut in a movie, and he had his parents move out to Los Angeles to join him since it seemed he finally made it in the movie industry.

But what was the end result of his debut? The movie turned out to be a failure. After that, he did not have any other opportunities. Jim had to ask his parents to leave Los Angeles due to his once again impoverished situation. Over the next 10 years, Jim worked and worked without earning any opportunities to showcase his talent again. Instead of giving up and switching professions, Jim worked on the miracle power of visualization. Even though he was now in his 20's and still had not experienced his dream of becoming an entertainer, his mind viewed him in a different universe. At night, Jim would drive up to the top of a hill near Los Angeles in his old car, and there he would calmly sit and envision himself being a success and landing lead roles in movies. After continuously doing this, he began to embody a belief that his visions were possible and that all he needed to do was continue working at his dream and one day he would no longer just be envisioning it up on that hill, he would be living it.

In 1990, over 11 years since he moved to Los Angeles without any real success, and over six years since his failed big screen debut, Jim wrote himself a check for $10,000,000 for acting services rendered, and he dated it Thanksgiving 1995. He then folded up the check and put it in his wallet.

When you write down your goals, you are putting it out in the universe. Something can be said of clearly defining what you want and writing it down. Think about whatever dream you have, and envision exactly what it is that you want. It cannot just be: "I want to be successful" – that is far too vague and there is no possible way of measuring when you have achieved it. Clearly define the success on a micro level, pinpointing the small details about it. If you aim small, you will miss small. For example, if a sniper in the military aims for just the overall body of his target, he will most likely miss the entire target. But if the sniper aims for the top button on his target's shirt and he is slightly off, he will still hit the target because he aimed for something very small. Write down a long-term goal of yours that is different than the current goal you already wrote down before. You do not need to share it with anyone. This is your goal, not your parents' goal, your friend's goal, or your teacher's goal. Save this slip somewhere where it will be safe, and years down the road, you can pull it out again when it has been achieved.

In 1994, Jim landed a lead role in the hit movie *Ace Ventura: Pet Detective*, and then followed it with another smash-hit movie

– *Dumb and Dumber*. He received over $10,000,000 from both of his acting roles in these comedies, and that little check he wrote himself five years prior for Thanksgiving 1995 had come to reality.

This legendary comedian and actor, Jim Carrey, continuously worked on improving his skill and in 1996, he received the largest amount of money for an acting role in a single movie in history at the time, which was $20,000,000. He made it onto *The Truman Show* in 1998 and won a Golden Globe award for Best Actor. Jim Carrey has performed numerous standup comedies that have been long-lasting hits, and he has continued to have leading roles in very popular movies such as *How the Grinch Stole Christmas*, which became the second highest grossing Christmas movie of all time, *Bruce Almighty*, which became the seventh highest grossing live-action comedy of all time, *Me Myself & Irene*, and the sequel *Dumb and Dumber To (2)*. Jim Carrey continues to appear in movies to this day, and he has been labeled as one of the biggest movie stars in all of Hollywood.

"You can fail at something you don't want, so you might as well take a chance on doing what you love."
– Jim Carrey

Chapter 16

Tom – Endless Failures

On an average day in February of 1847, an average boy named Tom entered this world. There was nothing special about him as a child, and actually, it seemed as if he was the complete opposite of the word "special."

Tom would begin school at the late age of seven in Michigan. While in class, he was often ridiculed by his teachers, and they labeled him as being mentally challenged with a lack of hope for a better future. Teachers play a critical role in the self-actualization process of a child, and the only beliefs Tom cultivated about himself were the negative remarks his teachers fed him. Teachers have the ability to positively or negatively impact the life of a child, acting in a sense like a parent away from home. His teachers also told him he was "too stupid to learn anything," and he was criticized for asking too many questions in class. Since Tom's forehead was unusually broad and his head was considered to be larger than normal, his teachers expressed that his brain was scrambled and that was why he was not an intelligent child. When Tom and his mother had a meeting with one of his teachers, the teacher told them that Tom did not have the ability to learn, so his mother took him out and decided he would be homeschooled.

Up until this point, Tom had only received negative feedback about himself as the school system basically wanted to kick him out for slowing down the betterment of the rest of the class. His capabilities and true intelligence always existed within him, but others could never see it. While his teachers viewed him asking questions as a sign of stupidity, questions actually demonstrate a sign of intellectual curiosity because if he did not have any interest in the subject being taught, he would never go through the trouble of asking questions. It is only through questions and challenging society's ways that we learn more about both the subject being taught and ourselves.

Since Tom was now being homeschooled, it was solely his own responsibility to become educated. He would not be competing against other students or have a teacher watching over his shoulder to ensure all assignments were completed to a specific standard, the only standard he would have is the one he holds himself to. Tom could have easily slacked off on his education while being at home and instead choose to sleep all day, because if he did, who was really going to know? But he set a higher standard for himself and embraced learning as much as he could.

At 10 years old in 1857, Tom built his first science laboratory in the basement of his family's home. Science had always intrigued Tom, and now having the opportunity to immerse himself in his studies at home, he would be able to generate his own experiments.

His father disapproved of all the time Tom would spend in the basement, which would be many hours in a week. With his parents being enthusiasts for reading books, Tom's father would offer him a penny (which had much more value back then) for each book he read in an attempt by his father to have Tom stop spending time on his science experiments.

While Tom profoundly enjoyed reading, his innate desire to experiment on his own outweighed his father's bribe to read books, an activity that he also truly enjoyed doing. Being a clever young boy, except in the eyes of the school system, Tom would accept his father's bribe and go read a book, which he could do rather quickly. With the penny now in hand, he would have the ability to buy more chemicals for his laboratory to conduct more experiments.

Books are one of the most powerful resources on this Earth as they can instantly change the circumstances of an individual by allowing him to acquire the knowledge needed to become more resourceful in his life. But equally as important as books are the experiences you will gain first hand in whatever task you immerse yourself in. The most resourceful and intelligent person is he who teaches himself how to excel at an endeavor on his own – matched with the vast knowledge of failures and successes he learns along the way.

In 1859, Tom accepted a low-paying job of selling candy and newspapers on a train. Eventually, Tom was able to move his home laboratory to a train baggage car after he received permission to do so. This privilege of his would soon be stripped away once he spilled chemicals in the baggage car and the lab caught fire. Tom and his chemicals were immediately thrown off the train for this disaster. Despite this calamity, Tom continued to pursue his passion of experimenting.

Throughout childhood, Tom often suffered from hearing problems, which began when he contracted scarlet fever. His deafness became worse later on due to an event that occurred in 1862. At 15 years old, Tom tried to jump on a moving train and the conductor grabbed his ears to help pull him onto the boxcar. Upon being pulled in, Tom felt something snap inside his head and he began to lose much of his hearing. He was completely deaf in his left ear, and he was 80 percent deaf in his right ear, so basically, Tom greatly struggled to hear at all.

Instead of feeling hopeless and accepting the many limitations in life that would come with losing his hearing, he chose to see what this deafness could possibly do to better his life. In any situation, no matter how bad it may seem, there is always something to gain from it. Nothing is either good or bad but it is our thinking that determines which way we want to perceive it. This means that no event in itself has positivity or negativity attached to it, but it is how we as individuals perceive this event that decides whether we view it as being something good or bad for us. How is it that two people could be in the exact same situation and one views the situation as being positive and the other views it as being negative? It is in the way they think that causes them to each view the same situation differently.

So how did Tom view his deafness? He turned his weakness, something no one would ever want to have happen, into an asset only he possessed. Tom said "Deafness probably drove me to reading." The ability to concentrate on his own thoughts without hearing all of the external noise provided him an opportunity to hone in on his reading and increase his knowledge. Losing one of the most important senses of the human body, Tom could have indulged in self-pity and despair, but he instead chose to turn it into a strength.

Tom would enter the telegraph business in 1863, after he saved a child from a runaway train whose father was in the telegraph business and offered to teach him about it. Tom would travel through large cities working on various telegraphing jobs, but he was often fired for misbehaving or failing to send and receive messages properly (which is what a telegraph does, it sends and receives messages on a device).

Upon his unsuccessful career working on telegraphing jobs around various large cities, Tom would soon move to Kentucky where he would be employed by Western Union. While under employment at the company, Tom would work the night shift so that he could spend time on his two main passions during the day, which were experimenting and reading.

How many of you would choose a night shift so that you can work on your passions during the day after working all night at your main job? Exhaustion and fatigue meant very little to Tom because doing scientific experiments and reading books meant so much more.

Only one year into his career at Western Union, Tom was threatened that he would be fired by the company for "not concentrating on his primary responsibilities and doing too much moonlighting." The company's threat actually came to fruition, when one night, Tom was working with lead-acid batteries at Western Union, and he spilled sulfuric acid onto the floor which leaked down onto his boss' desk from the ceiling above. The next day, Tom was fired.

First having to drop out of school for being "too stupid to learn anything," and now being fired from multiple jobs, many would say – can Tom do anything right? His legacy he would leave on the world was just beginning to show signs of life like molten lava deep inside a volcano seeping from the surface before an eruption.

Tom saw the first sign of success through an improvement he made to the stock ticker (although he is often cited as being the inventor). This major breakthrough had a very positive impact on society, and his confidence grew from this accomplishment. Among his most significant improvements to the stock ticker was a mechanism that synchronized all of the tickers on a line, so that when printed, it would show the same information.

With another idea in mind and needing money to develop it, Tom went about looking to sell his new invention for the stock ticker. He found a buyer for $10,000 (which was a considerable sum of money back then), and upon the success of his first invention, Tom had caught the "invention bug." His mind now began to see endless possibilities for all the things he could do. Having obtained the funds to pursue his next idea, Tom wanted to build a new science laboratory (like the one he had in his basement at home) that would produce constant inventions. In 1876, in the village of Menlo Park, New Jersey, Tom built what became known as the first industrial research lab, and citizens from all over became very intrigued by what Tom had built. Due to this new invention factory, Tom became known as "The Wizard of Menlo Park." Even with the level of success he now achieved between the improvement to the stock ticker and his industrial research lab, Tom wanted more.

You can never be satisfied with where you currently are because there is always more that you can achieve. That does not mean you should not be thankful for your accomplishments, but you should not become complacent and content with your current level of success; if you do, someone will surpass you. The inner drive to want more out of yourself and push yourself harder, even when you have achieved a level of success, is what pushes those that are "good" to become "great."

This continuous hunger allowed him to spend countless hours working on his next invention, which one year later would alter the world – the phonograph. This device recorded and reproduced sounds, and Tom demonstrated its abilities by singing to the phonograph "Mary Had a Little Lamb," and then it replayed his singing. Even though the phonograph was his best success up to this point in his life, he kept striving forward each day spending hours thinking and experimenting with new ideas.

Continuing with the momentum of his successful phonograph, Tom looked to pioneer an industry that was searching for a man with his type of character. Tom developed a work ethic that had a foundation forged from hard work and resiliency, and the failure that would occur on the way to his next invention only provided him with stronger reasons to continue pursuing it.

Tom, along with others at the time, realized that the current convention for generating electricity was inefficient and needed change. Most lighting was conducted through the use of either oil and gas or candles. An enormous opportunity existed for an individual that possessed the ability to creatively design a commercial light bulb that would last for hours and be inexpensive. The few others that came close to finding a solution could only design light bulbs that were either expensive or died very quickly and thus would not be adequate for use in society.

Wanting to learn as much as he could about electricity and the science behind it, Tom again submerged himself in his work. He made sacrifices no one else was willing to make and pushed himself through all mental barriers that tried to block him. With a determination to find a solution, Tom worked sometimes twenty hours a day trying to invent the commercial light bulb. He would only take small naps during the day because he wanted to get the most possible out of himself.

We have only 24 hours a day, but this is more than enough to get everything done. You do not maximize your 24 hours, which is why you complain you wish you had more time to get all your endeavors done. If we had 30 hours in a day, you would say the same exact thing: I wish I had more time in a day. So it is not the amount of time we are given, but rather what we do with that time. 24 hours is more than enough time – examine your day at night before you go to bed and you will realize just how many minutes or hours you waste engaging in useless activities.

Tom viewed sleep as being a waste of time, so he would often get only three to four hours of sleep a night. I am not saying whether you should follow this, that decision is yours, but this is the level of commitment you must have towards your dream in order to achieve a level of mastery. Instead of sleeping, Tom used these extra hours to gain a competitive advantage over the other equally bright scientists who were working on inventing the commercial light bulb as well.

Over and over Tom faced failure in his new invention, but he did not ever let the failure consume him. If he did, he would have never been one failed attempt closer to finally getting it right. All in all, Tom failed over 10,000 times trying to invent the lightbulb. Think of how profound that is – he failed over 10,000 times on one single idea! How many of you would have given up after only the first attempt?

Tom failed his way to success, and each failure showed him what does not work so that he knew to try something different the next time. If he never failed, he would have never known that the current method he was testing does not work – the possibility of that method working would have still existed and been undiscovered. So the only way he could prove that a particular method or material would not work was to test it and watch it fail.

After 10,000 failures, Tom finally struck success. The world was shaken in 1879 when Tom invented the first commercial light bulb, or modern electricity as we know it today. His name, Thomas Edison, soon became a phenomenon. He formed the Edison Electric Light Company, which later merged with another competitor, and the newly merged company became known as General Electric – currently one of the largest companies in the world.

Later in his life, he would also invent the motion picture which he worked on with his employee W.K.L Dickson. Numerous towns and schools have been named after Thomas Edison for all his contributions he made to modern society, and the highest honor awarded by the American Institute of Electrical Engineers is named after him – the Edison Medal.

Thomas Edison, one of the most common household names in society, began his life with the label of being an incompetent student unable to learn anything. After going deaf and being fired from numerous jobs, he pursued a challenging path as a daring inventor and faced thousands of failures. The grand level of success he eventually achieved in life was due to all the failures and struggles he overcame along the way and his drive to never surrender to any challenges.

"If we did all the things we are capable of,
we would literally astound ourselves."
– Thomas Edison

Chapter 17

Concluding Remarks

Congratulations on almost finishing this book, you should be very proud of yourself for taking action to invest in your mind in order to change your current situation. As you look to accomplish your goals, you will realize that the real value does not lie in actually achieving your goals, but in your journey of acquiring the knowledge and experience needed to achieve them. Knowledge and experience can never be taken from you, they are precious resources that can only be acquired one way, and that is through hard work and repeated failures. Let's say you are a very knowledgeable, successful, and wealthy person - if you are in a bizarre situation where you lose all your money, it will only be a matter of time before you earn that wealth again because you possess the knowledge in knowing how to properly acquire it - you already have the blueprint.

I would have loved to include more chapters for all the individuals who faced a myriad of failures and challenges and ultimately achieved grand success, but then this book would be written on almost the entire human history of all people who lived on this Earth. I chose these individuals that you just read about because I felt they represented a diverse sample of the population and each one faced unique challenges. All of these people were average individuals made of flesh and blood just like you, but they all shared the important quality – extraordinary work ethic. Greatness is not a gift and it is not something in our DNA, but rather greatness is a choice. It is the choice to make sacrifices others are not willing to make and to put everything you have into all of your endeavors. These individuals were fully committed to their endeavor, and they all gave up immediate gratification in order to achieve long-lasting success. A reputation is not built on what you say – it is built on what you do. The legacies these individuals in this book left behind were based on their actions. All of us are self-made, but only the successful will admit it.

Certain chapters in this novel may resonate with you more than others because they may relate more to your current situation. When things start to seem difficult and the dangerous thoughts of doubt and fear creep into your mind, it is critical that you re-read those meaningful chapters, or as I would advise, the entire book. When you read this book once, you will only retain some of the information, not all of it. When you read this book numerous times, you will pick up on things that you never did in your previous reads, similar to watching a comedy movie multiple times and later seeing certain scenes in a much funnier way. In addition, when you re-read this book at a later point in time, you will have acquired new information and experiences that can be applied or related to this book in a new way. Do not let this book sit on your shelf and collect dust, be proactive with it. Keep it near you at all times to remind you of the hidden secrets contained within it.

Whether you have just one major dream or many dreams, I cannot tell you enough that whatever it is you want to achieve, it is possible if you simply do not give up. Begin by changing your expectations for what you consider to be acceptable and not acceptable. You do not want to just be content with one great day, month, or year – you want to have a great life. Do not blame others for your lack of success because they have no bearing on what you can become, it is solely up to you to achieve your goal. No one is going to start that business for you, lose that weight for you, or study for you to pass that test, it is up to you to do it. And just because you are seeing no results now does not mean that is how your future will be; your results this year do not define your results next year. Here is a clear example of what most people do – let's say someone has been very overweight for 20 years and begins to workout and eat healthy, and their goal is to lose 100 pounds. After two months of following a workout and diet routine and having only lost 10 pounds, they are going to complain that they are not seeing any results and that it is not worth trying anymore. But does that person really expect two months of exercise and healthy eating to change 20 years of bad habits? Success is a process with no shortcuts. If you want to increase your results, then increase your input; it is a simple formula: your input = your output.

Depending on how old you currently are, go back either 5, 10, 20, or 50 years, and ask yourself this question: at that former age, would you be proud of your current life today? Is that where you would have wanted it to be? Would you be proud telling others at that former age that your current life today is what you dream of becoming? If not, do something today that your future self will thank you for when you engage in this thought process again some years from now.

Can you guess where the wealthiest place on Earth is? If you said anything that is related to gold, money, oil, or any other resource, you are wrong. The wealthiest place on this Earth is the graveyard. It is in the graveyard where there are buried dreams and aspirations that never came into existence because the people were too afraid to take the chance of pursuing them. All of these wonderful ideas, inventions, theories, businesses, and everything else inside of these individuals have died with them in the grave. They were never acted on or pursued, and now our whole world has to suffer the loss of these revolutionary ideas. Do not take your dreams and ideas with you to the grave to be forever lost.

I will leave you with this final thought to think about. On a tombstone, there is a date of birth, a date of death, and a dash in between the two. It is the dash that represents everything – the dash is the reason why people will visit your grave, mourn over your loss, and look up to you as inspiration in their own lives. What type of legacy will you leave in this dash?

Bibliography

"A Brief Biography of Thomas Edison." *National Parks Service*. U.S. Department of the Interior, 2014. Web. 7 Dec. 2014.

"A Resource Guide for Teachers of Educable Mentally Retarded Children." *State of Minnesota*. Department of Education, 1966. Web. 8 Jan. 2015.

"A Young Henry Ford – The Ford Story – Henry Ford Heritage Association." *Henry Ford Heritage Association*. HFHA, 2014. Web. 26 Dec. 2015.

"About Les Brown." *Les Bio*. Les Brown, Speak Your Way to Success!, 2014. Web. 21 Dec. 2014.

"About Us | Eric Thomas." Eric Thomas. 2014. Web. 8 Dec. 2014.

"Abraham Lincoln." *Bio*. A&E Networks Television, 2014. Web. 28 Dec. 2014.

"Abraham Lincoln." *History*. A&E Television Networks, 2015. Web. 8 Jan. 2015.

"Albert Einstein." *Bio*. A&E Television Networks, 2014. Web. 30 Nov. 2014.

"Albert Einstein." *Einstein*. Corbis Coporation, 2014. Web. 26 Nov. 2015.

"Albert Einstein." *History*. A&E Television Networks, 2014. Web. 26 Nov. 2015.

"Albert Einstein – Biographical". *Nobelprize.org*. Nobel Media AB 2014. Web. 26 Nov. 2014.

"American National Biography Online: Disney, Walt." *American National Biography Online*. Oxford University Press, 2000. Web. 2015.

"American National Biography Online: Lincoln, Abraham." *American National Biography Online*. Oxford University Press, 2015. Web. 8 Jan. 2015.

Beveridge, Mary. "What Is Walt Disney's Connection to Kansas City?" *The Kansas City Public Library*. The Kansas City Public Library, 1 Apr. 2006. Web. 4 Jan. 2015.

"Biography: Mariah Carey." *Lifetime*. A&E Television Network UK, 2014. Web. 30 Nov. 2014.

Birch, Nathan. "The Hard Rock Life: 10 True Facts About The Early Years Of Dwayne 'The Rock' Johnson." *The Hard Rock Life*. Uproxx, 9 Apr. 2015. Web. 28 May 2015.

Davidson, Jacob. "10 Things You Probably Didn't Know About Walt Disney." *TIME*. Time Inc., 16 Oct. 2013. Web. 8 May 2015.

"Dwayne Johnson – Biography." *IMDb*. IMDb.com, Inc., 2015. Web. 28 May 2015.

"Famous Quotes." *BrainyQuote*. BrainyQuote, 2015. Web. 8 Jan. 2015.

Griffin, Leslie. "Native Detroiter Eric Thomas Is a Motivational Master." *BLAC Detroit*. Metro Parent Publishing Group, 1 Feb. 2013. Web. 3 Dec. 2014.

Groth, Aimee. "Einstein's 23 Biggest Mistakes." *Business Insider*. Business Insider, Inc, 25 July 2011. Web.

"Henry Ford." *Bio*. A&E Networks Television, 2014. Web. 26 Dec. 2014.

"Henry Ford." *History*. A&E Television Networks, 2014. Web. 27 Dec. 2014.

"Hershey, PA: Who is Hershey Entertainment & Resorts?" *Hershey: The Sweetest Place on Earth*. Hershey, 2015. Web. 6 Jan. 2015.

"Howard Schultz." *Bio*. A&E Television Networks, 2014. Web. 29 Nov. 2014.

"Howard Schultz." *Forbes*. Forbes, 2014. Web. 29 Nov. 2014.

"Howard Schultz." *Starbucks Newsroom*. Starbucks, 2014. Web. 28 Nov. 2014.

"I'm the One – Les Brown." *YouTube*. YouTube, 2 Oct. 2014. Web. 19 Dec. 2014.

"It's Not OVER Until You Win! Your Dream Is Possible – Les Brown." *YouTube*. YouTube, 12 Aug. 2013. Web. 14 Dec. 2014.

"Jim Carrey – Biography." *Bio*. A&E Networks Television, 2015. Web. 19 May 2015.

"Jim Carrey – Biography." *IMDb*. IMDb.com, Inc., 2015. Web. 19 May 2015.

"Jim Carrey – Biography." *TalkTalk*. TalkTalk, 2015. Web. 19 May 2015.

"Jim Carrey – Biography." *The New York Times*. The New York Times Company, 2015. Web. 18 May 2015.

"J.K. Rowling." *J.K. Rowling*. TM Warner Bros. Entertainment Inc., 2012. Web. 21 May 2015.

"J.K. Rowling – Biography." *Bio*. A&E Networks Television, 2015. Web. 20 May 2015.

Lambert, Molly. "Started From the Bottom, Now He's the Rock ... and Other Inspirational Tales From This Week's Tabloids." *Grantland*. ESPN Internet Ventures, 25 Apr. 2013. Web. 28 May 2015.

Langer, Mark. "Disney, Walt." *American National Biography Online: Disney, Walt*. American National Biography Online, 1 Feb. 2000. Web. 4 Jan. 2015.

Lebowitz, Shana. "From the Projects to a $2.3 Billion Fortune – the Inspiring Rags-to-Riches Story of Starbucks CEO Howard Schultz." *Business Insider*. Business Insider, Inc., 30 May 2015. Web. 2 Jun. 2015.

"Les Brown." *Hour of Power: Guest Interviews: Les Brown*. Crystal Cathedral Ministries, 2014. Web. 24 Dec. 2014.

"Les Brown." *Les Brown | Bio | Premiere Motivational Speakers Bureau*. Premiere Speakers Bureau, 2014. Web. 14 Dec. 2014.

"Les Brown Author and Motivational Speaker – Biography." *Les Brown Biography*. American Speakers Bureau Coporation, 2014. Web. 30 Nov. 2014.

"Mariah Carey." *Bio*. A&E Networks Television, 2014. Web. 30 Nov. 2014.

"Mariah Carey." *Rolling Stone*. Rolling Stone, 2015. Web. 4 Jan. 2015.

"Mariah Carey's Biography." *Fox News*. FOX News Network, 24 Mar. 2008. Web. 2 Jan. 2015.

Merrill, Elizabeth. "12 Things to Know about Tom Brady." *ESPN*. ESPN, 1 Feb. 2012. Web. 28 Nov. 2014.

"Michael Jordan – Biography." *Bio*. A&E Networks Television, 2014. Web. 26 Nov. 2014.

"Milton Hershey Biography." *Bio*. A&E Networks Television, 2015. Web. 5 Jan. 2015.

"Milton S. Hershey." *Entrepreneur*. Entrepreneur, 7 Oct. 2008. Web. 6 Jan. 2015.

"Milton S. Hershey." *Milton Hershey School*. 2014. Web. 6 Jan. 2015.

"Milton S. Hershey." *The Hershey Company*. The Hershey Company, 2015. Web. 5 Jan. 2015.

"Milton Snavely Hershey Quotes." *Quoteswise*. Quoteswise, 2015. Web. 7 Jan. 2015.

Moynihan, Rob. "Dwayne Johnson Wrestles With His Most Personal Role Yet on HBO's Ballers." *TV Insider*. TV Insider LLC, 9 June 2015. Web. 5 June 2015.

"NBA.com: Michael Jordan Bio." NBA. NBA Media Ventures, LLC, 2014. Web. 27 Nov. 2014.

Nix, Elizabeth. "7 Things You May Not Know About Walt Disney." *History.com*. A&E Television Networks, 24 Feb. 2015. Web. 16 May 2015.

Ozanian, Mike. "Michael Jordan Is A Billionaire After Increasing Stake In Hornets." *Forbes*. Forbes Magazine, 12 June 2014. Web. 26 Nov. 2014.

"Price and Sales of Model T Ford Chart." *Federal Reserve Bank of Richmond*. Federal Reserve Bank of Richmond, 2014. Web. 28 Dec. 2014.

Redd, Nola. "Einstein's Theory of General Relativity." *SPACE.com*. SPACE.com, 15 Apr. 2015. Web. 2 June 2015.

Rothman, Michael. "Jim Carrey Reveals His Father's Failure Inspired His Comedic Dreams." *ABC News*. ABC News Network, 27 May 2014. Web. 18 May 2015.

Schlossberg, Mallory. "How Dwayne 'The Rock' Johnson Went from WWE Wrestler to Hollywood's Box-Office Champ." *Business Insider*. Business Insider, Inc., 5 Mar. 2015. Web. 30 May 2015.

The Brady 6. ESPN, 2011. Film.

"Thomas Edison – Biography." *Bio*. A&E Networks Television, 2014. Web. 10 Dec. 2014.

"Thomas Edison – Inventions." *History*. A&E Television Networks, 2015. Web. 7 Dec. 2014.

Thomas, Eric. "ERIC THOMAS | NOTHING TO SOMETHING." *YouTube*. Youtube, 8 May 2013. Web. 3 Dec. 2014.

"Timeline: Thomas Edison's Life." *PBS*. PBS, 2013. Web. 10 Dec. 2014.

"Tom Brady." *Bio*. A&E Television Networks, 2014. Web. 28 Nov. 2014.

"Tom Brady Biography." *JockBio*. Black Book Partners, 2012. Web. 28 Nov. 2014.

"Walt Disney." *Bio*. A&E Networks Television, 2015. Web. 2 Jan. 2015.

"Walt Disney." *IMDb*. IMDb.com, 2015. Web. 4 Jan. 2015.

"Walt Disney Biography: The Man Who Believed in Dreams." *Astrum People*. Astrum People, 2015. Web. 4 Jan. 2015.

45141270R00094

Made in the USA
Charleston, SC
12 August 2015